THE FEW
AND
THE MANY:

*Uncommon Readings
in American
Politics*

Poets 171

THE FEW
AND
THE MANY:

*Uncommon Readings
in American
Politics*

Edited by

Thomas R. Dye

*The Florida State
University*

L. Harmon Zeigler

*University of
Oregon*

DUXBURY PRESS

*A Division of
Wadsworth Publishing
Company, Inc.*

Belmont, California

1972

DUXBURY PRESS

*A Division of
Wadsworth Publishing
Company, Inc.*

Belmont, California

*L.C. Cat. Card No.: 73-184483
ISBN 0-87872-019-7*

Printed in the United States of America

1 2 3 4 5 6 7 8 9 10 _____ 76 75 74 73 72

Contents

Prefatory Note

THE FEW AND THE MANY is a carefully screened selection of what we feel is the best and most readable literature on elite-mass interaction as it is pertinent to the teaching of American politics at the introductory level. Although the volume is edited to have a life of its own, the organization parallels the framework of our text, *THE IRONY OF DEMOCRACY: An Uncommon Introduction to American Politics, 2nd edition* (Duxbury Press, 1972); and contains a representative sampling of the literature cited there. It would therefore serve as an effective complement to that text; or, independently, as a useful supplement in courses in which the instructor chooses to delve less deeply into an explanation of American political life from an *elite theory* perspective.

We are grateful to Robert Lineberry, of the University of Texas, among others, for his helpful criticisms of our manuscript at an earlier stage.

Acknowledgements for reprint rights on the selections which appear in this volume are to be found on pages 295–297.

1

**The Few and
the Many**

Our Founding Fathers were political realists. They were committed to the values of liberty and property, believed that all men were equal before the law, and believed that the legitimacy of any government should rest ultimately with the people themselves. But they did not permit these values to obscure their understanding of political reality.

Alexander Hamilton expressed the wisdom of the nation's founders when he wrote:

> All communities divide themselves into the few and the many. The first are the rich and the well-born, the other the masses of people. The voice of the people has been said to be the voice of God; and however generally this maxim has been quoted and believed, it is not true in fact. The people are turbulent and changing; they seldom judge or determine right. Give therefore to the first class a distinct, permanent share in the government. They will check the unsteadiness of the second, and as they cannot receive any advantage by change, they therefore will ever maintain good government.

Today it would be astounding to hear such words from any of the nation's leading statesmen, for Hamilton's views are clearly *elitist*. Today, the myths, symbols, and rhetoric of American politics are drawn from a *democratic* ideology. We talk of government "by the people," and we praise the virtue, wisdom, and good sense of the common man.

But is it possible that Hamilton's views more accurately express the reality of American politics than current rhetoric? Is it possible that America *is* divided among the "few" who exercise power and the "many" who do not? Is it true that the few who have power are "rich and well-born": that they are drawn from the upper socio-economic strata of society and control its economic resources? Is it possible that the judgment of the people is "turbulent and changing," and that the people are *not* strongly committed to the values of life, liberty, and property? Are the few who govern more firmly committed than the masses to the principles of liberty, tolerance, human welfare, and individual dignity? Is it true that the governing few are more interested in maintaining and preserving "good government" than the mass of people? Very few political commentators or government textbooks bother to deal with the questions raised by Hamilton's elitist statement. Since Hamilton's day, Americans have been educated in the democratic and pluralist tradition, and they have come to accept without question the tenets of that tradition.

Hamilton's idea of the few and the many raises still other questions: How do "the few" acquire power? What is the relationship between wealth and political power? How open and accessible are "the few?" Can individuals move in and out of the ranks of "the few" depending on their activity and interest in public affairs, or are the ranks of "the few" closed to all but top corporate, financial, military, and government leaders? Do "the few" change over time? How widely is power shared? How much competition takes place among the governing few? Can "the many" through elections, party competition, and interest group activity hold "the few" accountable for their policy decisions? Does it make any real difference in the lives of "the many" which members of "the few" occupy formal government offices? How responsive are "the few" to the preferences of "the many"? How much influence do "the many" have over the policies decided by "the few"? Does public policy reflect the preferences of the masses, or are these preferences manipulated by the governing few?

This volume will present historical and social science literature which deals with these and similar questions posed by *elite theory*. We know that elite theory runs contrary to the symbols of American politics, but we want to learn whether it accurately describes the *realities* of the American political system.

The Meaning of Elitism

What is elite theory? Let us summarize some of the central ideas of elite theory in order to provide a general framework for understanding the readings in this book.

(1) Society is divided into the few who have power and the many who do not. In all societies only a small number of persons can make decisions for the larger group. But it is particularly true that in large, urban, industrial, bureaucratic, and technologically advanced societies, power is organized and concentrated in a small number of individuals who occupy the top positions in the corporate, financial, government and military organizations of society.

(2) The few who govern are not typical of the masses who are governed. Elites are drawn disproportionately from the upper socio-economic classes of society, and own or control a disproportionate share of societal structure—industry, commerce, finance, education, the military, communications, civic affairs, and law.

(3) The movement of non-elites to elite positions must be slow and continuous to maintain stability and avoid revolution. Only non-elites who have accepted the basic elite consensus can be admitted to governing circles. Elitism does *not* mean that individuals from the lower classes cannot rise to the top. In fact, a certain amount of "circulation of elites" (upward mobility) is essential for stability of the elite system. However, only those non-elites who have demonstrated their commitment to the values of the dominant elite can be trusted with power.

(4) Elites concur on the basic values of the social system and the importance of preserving the system. The range of issues on which they disagree is very narrow in comparison with the range of matters on which they agree.

(5) Public policy does not reflect demands of the masses but rather the prevailing values of the elite. Changes in public policy are incremental rather than revolutionary, and come about when elites change their own values. These changes are slow and marginal rather than rapid and revolutionary.

(6) Elites are subject to relatively little direct influence from the masses, which are largely passive, apathetic, and ill-informed. Mass sentiments are manipulated by elites more often than elite values are influenced by mass sentiments. Democratic institutions, elections, parties, and interest groups, are important primarily for their symbolic value—they help tie the masses to the political system—hence the masses have, at best, only an indirect influence over the decisions of the elite.

Elitism is not a conspiracy to oppress or exploit the masses. On the contrary, elites may be very "public-spirited" and deeply concerned with the welfare of the masses. Elitism does not pretend that power in society does not shift over time or that new elites cannot emerge to compete with old elites. It does not mean that there is never *any* competition among elite members (indeed, elite competition may be very bitter at times), but that elite competition occurs over the means rather than the ends of public policy. Elitism does not mean that power rests exclusively with those who control the economic resources of society, but it may also rest upon other resources, organization, communication, and information. Elitism does not mean that the masses *never* have any impact on the attitudes of elites, only that elites influence masses more than masses influence elites.

Most Americans are more familiar with democratic theory than with elite theory. Democracy means participation in the decisions that shape one's life. All democrats have endorsed the idea of some form of popular participation in societal decision-making. Democracy also means a commitment to individual dignity and the preservation of the liberal values of life, liberty, and property. These rights are inalienable; they were not given to individuals by governments, and no government may legitimately take them away. Democracy also means equal opportunity for all men to develop their individual capacities. This means an equal opportunity to influence public policy, and it also means equality of opportunity in all aspects of American life—social, educational, and economic, as well as political.

The Meaning of Pluralism

Despite political rhetoric in America concerning citizen participation in decision-making, majority rule, our protection of minorities, individual rights, and equality of opportunity, no scholar or commentator, however optimistic about life in this country, would contend that these conditions have been fully realized in the American political system. No one contends that citizens participate in *all* the decisions which shape their lives, or that majority preferences *always* prevail. Nor do they argue that the rights of minorities are *always* protected, or that the values of life, liberty, and property are *never* sacrificed, or that *every* American has an equal opportunity to influence public policy. But modern *pluralism* does seek to reaffirm the democratic character of American society by contending that:

(1) Although citizens do not directly participate in decision-making, their many leaders do make decisions through a process of bargaining, accommodation, and compromise.

(2) There is competition among leadership groups which helps to protect the interests of individuals. Countervailing centers of power—for example, competition between business leaders, labor leaders, and governmental leaders—can check each other and keep each interest from abusing its power and oppressing the individual.

(3) Individuals can influence public policy by choosing between competing elites in elections. Elections and parties allow individuals to hold leaders accountable for their action.

(4) While individuals do not participate directly in decision-making, they can join organized groups and make their influence felt through their participation in these organizations.

(5) Leadership groups are not closed; new groups can be formed and gain access to the political system.

(6) Although political influence in society is unequal, power is widely dispersed. Frequently, access to decision-making is based on the level of interest people have in a particular decision, and because leadership is fluid and mobile, power depends upon one's interest in public affairs, skills in leadership, information about issues, knowledge of democratic processes, and skill in organization and public relations.

(7) There are multiple leadership groups within society. Those who exercise power in one kind of decision do not necessarily exercise power in others. No single elite dominates decision-making in all issue areas.

(8) Public policy is not necessarily majority preference, but it is an equilibrium of interest interaction. Such equilibrium is the approximate balance of competing interest group influences and is therefore a reasonable approximation of society's preferences.

Frequently confusion arises in distinguishing *pluralism* from *elitism.* Pluralists *say* that the system they describe is a reaffirmation of democratic theory in a modern, urban, industrial society. They offer pluralism as "a practical solution" to the problem of achieving democratic ideals in a large complex social system where direct individual participation and decision-making is simply not possible. But many critics of pluralism assert that it is a covert form of elitism—they accuse the pluralists of being closer to the elitist position than to the democratic tradition which they revere. Thus, political scientist Peter Bachrach has described pluralism as "democratic elitism."

Until quite recently democratic and elite theories were regarded as distinct and conflicting. While in their pure form they are still regarded as contradictory, there is, I believe, a strong if not dominant trend in contemporary public thought incorporating major elitist principles within democratic theory. As a result there is a new theory which I have called democratic elitism.

But pluralism does diverge from democracy in at least the following respects: (a) decisions are made by elite interaction—bargaining, accommodation, and compromise—rather than by direct individual participation. At best, individuals are given only an indirect role in the political system. The key political actors are leaders of institutions and organizations rather than individual citizens; (b) even if power is fragmented among multiple elites as pluralists claim, this does not ensure political equality. Inequality of power among interests is commonplace, and it is usually the producer interests, bound together by economic ties, which eventually dominate the less organized consumer groups; (c) pluralists contend that power is distributed among governmental and nongovernmental institutions and organizations, but there is ample evidence that these institutions are governed by small groups of leaders (oligarchies) rather than by their members; (d) and finally, pluralists assume that institutions and organizations which divide power will compete among themselves. But is there any real reason why they should? If different groups of leaders make decisions in different issue areas, it seems likely that each group would allow every other group to govern within its own sphere of influence. Accommodation, rather than competition, may be the prevailing style of elite interaction.

Elitism in American Politics

Elitism asserts that society is divided among the few who have power and the many who do not. The powerful few are not typical of the masses in either background or attitude. They are drawn disproportionately from the upper socio-economic strata of society and are in a position to control societal resources. These few also share a consensus which favors the interests of basic elites rather than demands of masses. Elitism proposes that changes in public policy are incremental rather than revolutionary, and that the movement of non-elites into elite positions is slow and limited only to non-elites who have accepted elite values. Finally, elitism argues that elites influence masses more than masses influence elites.

In contrast, *pluralism* is a belief that democratic values can be preserved in an urban, industrial, technological society by a system of multiple competing elites among whom power is fragmented and diffused. It asserts that non-elites can become elites by becoming active in public affairs and by acquiring information about issues, knowledge about democratic processes, and skill in leadership, organization, and public relations. Pluralism notes that voters can influence public policy by choosing between competing elites in elections, and that the party system allows effective policy choice. Masses also exercise influence over elites through membership in organizations which are active in public affairs and have sufficient power to hold elites accountable for their decisions. Pluralism defends the concept of competition among elites and the belief that different elites govern in different issue areas, hence no single elite can dominate decision-making in society.

The readings in this volume will help us to evaluate elitism and pluralism as descriptive models of the American political system. In Chapter 1 we will explore the meaning of each term as it is defined in the literature of political theory. Our selections are by Gaetano Mosca, Thomas Jefferson, Robert Dahl, and Peter Bachrach. In Chapter 2 we examine the political thought of the Founding Fathers as reflected in the writings of James Madison, and then observe the nation's first elite in their task of Constitution writing through the eyes of two historians, Charles Beard and Richard Hofsteader. Contemporary American elites—corporate, financial, governmental, and military—are described in Chapter 3 in the writings of C. Wright Mills, Arthur M. Louis, John K. Galbraith, Donald Matthews, and Morris Janowitz; and mass attitudes and behaviors in Chapter 4 by a group of social scientists. The effectiveness of parties and elections as instruments of popular control over government and public policy are then reviewed in the writings of Roberto Michaels, Gerald Pomper, Edward C. Banfield, Murray Edelman, Donald Matthews, and James Prothro. In Chapter 6, we look at our national government elites, the President, Congress, and the Supreme Court.

The literature on power in specific communities has contributed very significantly to understanding the general nature of power, elections, and democracy in America. Our readings include excerpts from two of the most influential community power studies: Floyd Hunter's study of Atlanta, Georgia, and Robert Dahl's study of New Haven, Connecticut. We have included as well a general evaluation of this literature by John Walton.

The final two Chapters, 8 and 9, are attempts to describe elite behavior in relation to two nationally important subjects, civil rights and urban violence. The civil rights movement began well within the established elite philosophy of equality of opportunity, and the movement has operated well within the established rules for change. Its principal tactic, nonviolent direct action, is essentially a dramatic form of appeal to the underlying sentiments of established elites. It has not attempted to replace established elites or restructure societal values; rather, it has asked elites to permit blacks to *share* in the established system. Martin Luther King's famous "Letter from Birmingham Jail" conveys the extent to which the civil rights movement began with accepted values and appealed to the conscience of white elites. President Lyndon Johnson's Howard University speech in 1965 indicated that at that time national elites were committed to equality of opportunity, supported the removal of legal barriers to equal opportunity, and even realized that removing legal barriers could not ensure equal opportunity. To conclude Chapter 8, Bayard Rustin and Stokeley Carmichael debate the utility of black coalition with established political forces in America.

Violence has been common in American history. No major social movement of the last 200 years has been free of it. It would be unrealistic to hope that the black struggle in America would not engender violence among both black and white masses. In Chapter 10 H. Rap Brown demands absolute equality—now— and he suggests force as a means of obtaining it. Compare this point of view with that expressed in the report published by the National Commission on Civil Disorders, where elites uniformly condemn violence as a means of change.

The selections end with a marvelous essay by Aaron Wildavsky, which exposes the exquisite dilemma of the liberal elite. Having encouraged the black masses to believe that progress is possible and that political activity can be effective, they are dismayed to see these same masses indeed undertake to secure the good things in life without much regard for the established rules of the system.

How America is Ruled:
Elitism, Pluralism, and
Democracy

Political scientist Harold Lasswell once observed: "Government is always government by the few, whether in the name of the few, the one, or the many." In America, of course, the few govern in the name of the many. Hence the confusion between the symbolism and the reality of American politics.

Our first set of readings is drawn from the works of political philosophers. Political philosophy concerns itself with the ways in which man can and should be governed. It *describes* the nature of man and society, and also *prescribes* the way in which men ought to govern themselves. Generally the political philosopher's view of the nature of man in society is closely related to his recommendations for good government. That is to say, description and prescription are closely related. Traditionally, democratic philosophers have described man as basically virtuous, reasonable, wise, and capable of self-government. Elitist philosophers, on the other hand, have frequently been less generous in their evaluation of the common man's intelligence, virtue, and reason, and therefore they have had less confidence in government by the masses. Moreover, elitists also assert that no society can be governed by anything other than a *minority* of its members. Even if it were desirable, Democracy would be a practical impossibility.

One of the classic statements of elitist philosophy was written in 1896: *The Ruling Class, Elemente de Scienza Politica*, by Italian social scientist Gaetano Mosca. In this influential book, Mosca set forth his reasons for believing that all societies divide themselves into "a class that rules and a class that is ruled." He viewed elitism as a logical necessity in any social organization. Separate individuals cannot govern a social system. An organized group is always more powerful than a single man, so there will always be an incentive for minorities to organize themselves in order to gain power. Mosca also argued that these minorities "are usually so constituted that the individuals that make them up are distinguished from the mass of the governed." They possess or are attributed certain qualities which make them "highly esteemed and very influential."

Mosca was not only a political philosopher but also a distinguished member of the Italian Senate in the 1920's. It should come as no surprise that Mosca's political career was ended abruptly when he tried to defend traditional values against a mass-supported popular demagogue of his times, Benito Mussolini.

In defense of the philosophy of the common man, we have selected two letters by America's most gifted and revered democrat, Thomas Jefferson. In the first, a letter to a member of one of America's most distinguished elite families, DuPont de Nemours, Jefferson expresses the democrat's confidence in the judgment of the masses: "We both consider the people as our children, and love them with parental affection. But you love them as infants whom you are afraid to trust without nurses, and I as adults, who I freely leave to self-government." Note that Jefferson does not attack his elitist friend as either oppressive or exploitive. He realizes than an elitist may have a deep love and affection for the people. But he believes that the people can govern themselves and preserve the values of life, liberty, and property—if they are given the proper means for doing so. The key is education, and his confidence in it is unbounded: "Enlighten the people generally, and tyranny and oppressions of body and mind will vanish like evil spirits at the dawn of day." If the people are properly educated, he says, they can govern themselves. In the second letter, to another member of a great American elite family, John Adams, Jefferson expands this thesis, arguing convincingly that "artificial aristocracy," or "pseudo-aristocracy," must give way to a natural aristocracy based upon educational accomplishment in free public schools.

In defense of modern American pluralism, we have selected a brief excerpt from Robert A. Dahl's *Pluralist Democracy in the United States.* Professor Dahl is a past president of the American Political Science Association and a former chairman of the Department of Political Science at Yale University. It is thus appropriate that he be the leading exponent of the "established" political philosophy in America. Professor Dahl is sensitive to the complex problems of self-government; he understands the ambiguity of the phrase, "the people," and the serious difficulties in implementing majority rule. Yet he reaffirms the survival of the democratic tradition in America, and he sets forth "a pluralist solution" to the problem of popular government in modern society. His pluralist solution encompasses (a) a sense of national identity, (b) constitutional guarantees of personal liberty, (c) the widespread distribution of power among different segments of society, and (d) competition, negotiation, and bargaining among diverse interests in the making of public policy. He asserts that pluralism can be an effective means of achieving democracy in a modern and complex society and contends that pluralism is, in fact, the prevailing style of politics in America today.

A generation or more of Americans have been educated in the pluralist ideology. In recent years, however, a number of scholars have challenged the assertion that individuals can effectively participate in the decisions which shape their lives in a pluralist system and have also undermined the claim that the American system is in fact pluralistic. These scholars are sometimes referred to as "neo-elitists." They perceive an essentially elitist structure of power in America rather than a pluralist one, and they accuse pluralists of being less democratic than they claim. One of the leading neo-elitist critics is Peter Bachrach, and we have selected a portion of his influential book, *The Theory of Democratic Elitism*, to represent this viewpoint. The article reviews the growing disenchantment with the common man among pluralist scholars. While Bachrach himself is personally opposed to elitism, he carefully describes why the common man, within the context of the present system, is not strongly committed to the values of liberty, equality, and democracy. Thus, Bachrach finds himself in the dilemma of many neo-elitists; while he objects to the current system of elite governance in America, he also acknowledges that the masses cannot be trusted to preserve democratic values.

Power and Elites
Gaetano Mosca

Among the constant facts and tendencies that are to be found in all political organisms, one is so obvious that it is apparent to the most casual eye. In all societies—from societies that are very meagerly developed and have barely attained the dawnings of civilization, down to the most advanced and powerful societies—two classes of people appear—a class that rules and a class that is ruled. The first class, always the less numerous, performs all political functions, monopolizes power and enjoys the advantages that power brings, whereas the second, the more numerous class, is directed and controlled by the first, in a manner that is now more or less legal, now more or less arbitrary and violent, and supplies the first, in appearance at least, with material means of subsistence and with the instrumentalities that are essential to the vitality of the political organism.

In practical life we all recognize the existence of this ruling class. . . . We all know that, in our own country, whichever it may be, the management of public affairs is in the hands of a minority of influential persons, to which management, willingly or unwillingly, the majority defer. We know that the same thing goes on in neighboring countries, and in fact we should be put to it to conceive of a real world otherwise organized—a world in which all men would be directly subject to a single person without relationships of superiority or subordination, or in which all men would share equally in the direction of political affairs. If we reason otherwise in theory, that is due partly to inveterate habits that we follow in our thinking and partly to the exaggerated importance that we attach to two political facts that loom far larger in appearance than they are in reality.

The first of these facts—and one has only to open one's eyes to see it—is that in every political organism there is one individual who is chief among the leaders of the ruling class as a whole and stands, as we say, at the helm of the state. That person is not always the person who holds supreme power according to law. At times, alongside of the hereditary king or emperor there is a prime minister or a major-domo who wields an actual power that is greater than the sovereign's. At other times, in place of the elected president the influential politician who has procured the president's election will govern. Under special circumstances there may be, instead of a single person, two or three who discharge the functions of supreme control.

The second fact, too, is readily discernible. Whatever the type of political organization, pressures arising from the discontent of the masses who are governed, from the passions by which they are swayed, exert a certain amount of influence on the policies of the ruling, the political, class.

But the man who is at the head of the state would certainly not be able to govern without the support of a numerous class to enforce respect for his orders and to have them carried out; and granting that he can make one individual, or indeed many individuals, in the ruling class feel the weight of his power, he certainly cannot be at odds with the class as a whole or do away with it. Even if that were possible, he would at once be forced to create another class, without the support of which action on his part would be completely paralyzed. On the other hand, granting that the discontent of the masses might succeed in deposing a ruling class, inevitably, as we shall later show, there would have to be another organized minority within the masses themselves to discharge the functions of a ruling class. Otherwise all organization, and the whole social structure, would be destroyed.

From the point of view of scientific research the real superiority of the concept of the ruling, or political, class lies in the fact that the varying structure of ruling classes has a preponderant importance in determining the political type, and also the level of civilization, of the different peoples. According to a manner of classifying forms of government that is still in vogue, Turkey and Russia were both, up to a few years ago, absolute monarchies, England and Italy were constitutional, or limited, monarchies, and France and the United States were classed as republics. The classification was based on the fact that, in the first two countries mentioned, headship in the state was hereditary and the chief was nominally omnipotent; in the second two, his office is hereditary but his powers and prerogatives are limited; in the last two, he is elected.

That classification is obviously superficial. Absolutisms though they were, there was little in common between the manners in which Russia and Turkey were managed politically, the levels of civilization in the two countries and the organization of their ruling classes being vastly different. On the same basis, the regime in Italy, a monarchy, is much more similar to the regime in France, a Republic, than it is to the regime in England, also a monarchy; and there are important differences between the political organizations of the United States and France, though both countries are republics.

As we have already suggested, ingrained habits of thinking have long stood, as they still stand, in the way of scientific progress in this matter. The classification mentioned above, which divides governments into absolute monarchies, limited monarchies and republics, was devised by Montesquieu and was intended to replace the classical categories of Aristotle, who divided governments into monarchies, aristocracies and democracies. What Aristotle called a democracy was simply an aristocracy of fairly broad membership. Aristotle himself was in a position to observe that in every Greek state, whether aristocratic or democratic, there was always one person or more who had a preponderant influence. Between the day of Polybius and the day of Montesquieu, many writers perfected Aristotle's classification by introducing into it the concept of "mixed" governments. Later on the modern democratic theory, which had its source in Rousseau, took its stand upon the concept that the majority of the citizens in any state can participate, and in fact *ought* to participate, in its political life, and the doctrine of popular sovereignty still holds sway over many minds in spite of the fact that modern scholarship is making it increasingly clear that democratic, monarchical and aristocratic principles function side by side in every political organism. We shall not stop to refute this democratic theory here, since that is the task of this work as a whole. Besides, it would be hard to destroy in a few pages a whole system of ideas that has become firmly rooted in the human mind. . . .

We think it may be desirable, nevertheless, to reply at this point to an objection which might very readily be made to our point of view. If it is easy to understand that a single individual cannot command a group without finding within the group a minority to support him, it is rather difficult to grant, as a constant and natural fact, that minorities rule majorities, rather than majorities minorities. But that is one of the points—so numerous in all the other sciences—where the first impression one has of things is contrary to what they are in reality. In reality the dominion of an organized minority, obeying a single impulse, over the unorganized majority is inevitable. The power of any minority is irresistible as against each single individual in the majority, who stands alone before the totality of the organized minority. At the same time, the minority is organized for the very reason that it is a minority. A hundred men acting uniformly in concert, with a common understanding, will triumph over a thousand men who are not in accord and can therefore be dealt with one by one. Meanwhile it will be easier for the former to act in concert and have a mutual understanding simply because they are a hundred and not a thousand. It follows that the larger the political community, the smaller will the proportion of the governing minority to the governed majority be, and the more difficult will it be for the majority to organize for reaction against the minority.

However, in addition to the great advantage accruing to them from the fact of being organized, ruling minorities are usually so constituted that the individuals who make them up are distinguished from the mass of the governed by qualities that give them a certain material, intellectual or even moral superiority; or else they are the heirs of individuals who possessed such qualities. In other words, members of a ruling minority regularly have some attribute, real or apparent, which is highly esteemed and very influential in the society in which they live.

. . .So far, in all the countries that have adopted universal suffrage more or less recently, the educated and well-to-do classes have maintained their rule under its aegis, though their influence has been tempered more or less by the influence of the petty bourgeoisie and of representatives of the interests of certain groups in the proletariat. That type of democracy is not so very different from the sort of government that Saint-Simon approved of and which he wanted Louis XVIII to use his authority to inaugurate—government by businessmen, scientists, scholars and artists. Democratic institutions may be able to endure for some time yet if, in virtue of them, a certain equilibrium between the various elements in the ruling class can be maintained, if our *apparent* democracy is not fatally carried away by logic, its worst enemy, and by the appetites of the lower classes and their leaders, and if it does not attempt to become *real* democracy by combining political equality with economic and cultural equality.

On the main intrinsic cause for the slight success that has so far been enjoyed by the doctrine that a ruling class necessarily exists, we have already touched very briefly.

A doctrine is a thread by which those who are examining a given body of facts try to guide themselves in the maze which the facts seem to present at first glance; and a doctrine becomes the more useful in practice the more it facilitates and simplifies the understanding and analysis of facts. In this matter of political theory, as in so many other matters, appearances are often as satisfactory to people as the substance would be. The old classifications of the various forms of government—the classification of Aristotle, who divided governments into monarchies, aristocracies and democracies, and the classification of Montesquieu, who trisected them into despotic, monarchical and republican governments—answered that purpose well enough. Following the Stagirite and the author of the *Esprit des lois,* anyone could get his bearings in political theory by deciding in just what category the government of his own country, or the governments of neighboring or even distant countries, belonged. Once that point was settled, he could well believe himself authorized to go on and point out the values, defects and dangers of this or that form of government, and to answer any objections that might be made to it by simply applying the precepts of the master he followed, or the master's successors.

On the other hand, merely to assert that in all forms of government the real and actual power resides in a ruling minority is to dismiss the old guides without supplying new ones—it is to establish a generic truth which does not take us at once into the heart of political happenings, present or past, and which does not explain by itself why certain political organisms are strong and others weak, nor suggest ways and means of preventing their decadence or repairing their defects. To assign all credit for the prosperity of a society, or all responsibility for its political decrepitude, to its ruling class is of little help when we do not know the various ways in which ruling classes are formed and organized. It is precisely in that variety of type that the secret of their strength and weakness must be sought and found.

The comprehensive and generic demonstration that a ruling class necessarily exists has to be supplemented, therefore, with an analytical study. We must patiently seek out the constant traits that various ruling classes possess and the variable traits with which the remote causes of their integration and solution, which contemporaries almost always fail to notice, are bound up. It is a question, after all, of using the procedure that is so much used in the natural sciences, in which no end of information that has now become an indestructible patrimony of human knowledge is due to happy intuitions, some of which have been confirmed, others modified, but all elaborated and developed by successive experiments and experiences. If it should be objected that it is difficult, and we might add, virtually impossible, to make experiments in cases where social phenomena are involved, one might answer that history, statistics and economics have by now gathered such a great store of experimental data that enough are available to permit us to begin our search.

Two Letters on Democracy

Thomas Jefferson

A Letter to Du Pont de Nemours

Poplar Forest, Apr. 24, 1816.

I received, my dear friend your letter covering the constitution of your Equinoctial republics, just as I was setting out for this place. I brought it with me, and have read it with great satisfaction. I suppose it well-formed for those for whom it is intended, and the excellence of every government is its adaptation to the state of those to be governed by it. For us it would not do. Distinguishing between the structure of the government and the moral principles on which you prescribe its administration, with the latter we concur cordially, with the former we should not. We of the United States, you know are constitutionally and conscientiously Democrats. We consider society as one of the natural wants with which man has been created; that he has been endowed with faculties and qualities to effect its satisfaction by concurrence of others having the same want; that when by the exercise of these faculties he has procured a state of society, it is one of his acquisitions which he has a right to regulate and controul, jointly indeed with all those who have concurred in the procurement, whom he cannot exclude from its use or direction more than they him. We think experience has proved it safer, for the mass of individuals composing the society, to reserve to themselves personally the exercise of all rightful powers to which they are competent, and to delegate those to which they are not competent to deputies named, and removable for unfaithful con-duct, by themselves immediately. Hence with us, the people (by which is meant the maŝs of individuals composing the society) being competent to judge of facts occurring in ordinary life, they have retained the functions of judges of facts, under the name of jurors; but being unqualified for the management of affairs requiring intelligence above the common level, yet competent judges of human character, they chuse for their management representatives, some by themselves immediately, others by electors chosen by themselves. Thus, our President is chosen by ourselves, directly *in practice,* for we vote for A. as elector only on the condition he will vote for B.; our representatives by ourselves immediately, our Senate and judges of the law through electors chosen by ourselves. And we believe that this proximate choice and power of removal is the best security which experi-ence has sanctioned for ensuring an honest conduct in the functionaries of the society. Your three or four alembications have indeed a seducing appearance. We should conceive prima facie, that the last extract would be the pure alcohol of the substance, three or four times rectified; but in proportion as they are more and more sublimated, they are also farther and farther removed from the controul of society, and human character, we believe, requires in general constant and immediate controul to prevent its being biassed from right by the seductions of self love. Your process produces, therefore, a structure of government from which the fundamental principle of ours is excluded. You first set as zeros all individuals not having lands, which are the greater number in every society of long standing. Those holding lands are permitted to manage in person the small affairs of their commune or corporation, and to elect a deputy for the canton; in which election, too, every one's vote is to be an unit, a plurality, or a fraction, in proportion to his landed possessions. The assem blies of Cantons then elect for the Districts, those of Districts for Circles, and those of Circles for the National assemblies. Some of these highest councils, too, are in a considerable degree self-elected, the regency partially, the judiciary entirely, and some are for life. Whenever, therefore, an esprit de corps, or of party, gets possession of them, which experience shows to be inevitable, there are no means of breaking it up; for they will never elect but those of their own spirit. Juries are allowed in criminal cases only.

I acknowledge myself strong affection for our own form. Yet both of us act and think from the same motive. We both consider the people as our children, and love them with parental affection. But you love them as infants whom you are afraid to trust without nurses, and I as adults, whom I freely leave to self government. And you are right in the case referred to you, my criticism being built on a state of society not under your contemplation. It is, in fact, like a critique on Homer by the laws of the Drama.

But when we come to the moral principles on which the government is to be administered, we come to what is proper for all conditions of society. I meet you there in all the benevolence and rectitude of your native character, and I love myself always most when I concur most with you. Liberty, truth, probity, honor are declared to be the four cardinal principles of your society. I believe with you that morality, compassion, generosity are innate elements of the human construction; that there exists a right independent of force; that a right to property is founded in our natural wants, in the means with which we were endowed to satisfy these wants, and the right to what we acquire by those means without violating the similar rights of other sensible beings; that no one has a right to obstruct another, exercising his faculties innocently for the relief of sensibilities made a part of his nature; that justice is the fundamental law of society; that the majority oppressing an individual, is guilty of crime, abuses its strength, and by acting on the law of the strongest, breaks up the foundations of society; that action by the citizens in person in affairs within their reach and competence, and in all other by representatives, chosen immediately and removable by themselves, constitutes the essence of a republic; that all governments are more or less republican in proportion as this principle enters more or less into their composition; and that a government by representation is capable of extension over a greater surface of country than one of any other form.

These, my friend, are the essentials in which you and I agree; however, in our zeal for their maintenance, we may be perplexed and divaricate, as to the structure of society most likely to secure them.

In the constitution of Spain as proposed by the late Cortes, there was a principle entirely new to me, and not noticed in yours, that no person, born after that day, should ever acquire the rights of citizenship until he could read and write. It is impossible sufficiently to estimate the wisdom of this provision. Of all those which have been thought of for securing fidelity in the administration of the government, constant ralliance to the principles of the constitution, and progressive amendments with the progressive advances of the human mind, or changes in human affairs, it is the most effectual. Enlighten the people generally, and tyranny and oppressions of body and mind will vanish like evil spirits at the dawn of day. Altho' I do not, with some enthusiasts, believe that the human condition will ever advance to such a state of perfection as that there shall no longer be pain or vice in the world, yet I believe it susceptible of much improvement, and, most of all, in matters of government and religion; and that the diffusion of knowledge among the people is to be the instrument by which it is to be effected. The constitution of the Cortes had defects enough; but when I saw in it this amendatory provision I was satisfied all would come right in time, under its salutary operation. No people have more need of a similar provision than those for whom you have felt so much interest. No mortal wishes them more success than I do, but if what I have heard of the ignorance and bigotry of the mass be true, I doubt their capacity to understand and to support a free government, and fear their emancipation from the foreign tyranny of Spain will result in a military despotism at home. Palacios may be great; others may be great; but it is the multitude which possesses force; and wisdom must yield to that. For such a condition of society, the constitution you have devised is probably the best imaginable. It is certainly calculated to elicit the best talents, altho', perhaps, not well guarded against the egoism of its functionaries, but that egoism will be light in comparison with the pressure of a military despot, and his army of Janissaries. Like Solon to the Athenians, you have given to your Columbians, not the best possible government, but the best they can bear. By-the-bye, I wish you had called them the Columbian republics, to distinguish them from our American republics. Theirs would be the more honorable name, and they best entitled to it; for Columbus discovered their continent, but never saw ours.

To them liberty and happiness; to you the meed of wisdom and goodness in teaching them how to attain them, with the affectionate respect and friendship of Th. J.

From A Letter to John Adams

Monticello, Oct. 28, 1813.

. . . I agree with you that there is a natural aristocracy among men. The grounds of this are virtue and talents. Formerly, bodily powers gave place among the aristoi. But since the invention of gunpowder has armed the weak as well as the strong with missile death, bodily strength, like beauty, good humor, politeness and other accomplishments, has become but an auxiliary ground for distinction. There is also an artificial aristocracy, founded on wealth and birth, without either virtue or talents; for with these it would belong to the first class. The natural aristocracy I consider as the most precious gift of nature, for the instruction, the trusts, and government of society. And indeed, it would have been inconsistent in creation to have formed man for the social state, and not to have provided virtue and wisdom enough to manage the concerns of the society. May we not even say, that that form of government is the best, which provides the most effectually for a pure selection of these natural aristoi into the offices of government? The artificial aristocracy is a mischievous ingredient in government, and provision should be made to prevent its ascendency. On the question, what is the best provision, you and I differ; but we differ as rational friends, using the free exercise of our own reason, and mutually indulging its errors. You think it best to put the pseudo-aristoi into separate chamber of legislation, where they may be hindered from doing mischief by their co-ordinate branches and where, also, they may be a protection to wealth against the Agrarian and plundering enterprises of the majority of the people. I think that to give them power in order to prevent them from doing mischief, is arming them for it, and increasing instead of remedying the evil. For if the co-ordinate branches can arrest their action, so may they that of the co-ordinates. Mischief may be done negatively as well as positively. Of this, a cabal in the Senate of the United States has furnished many proofs. Nor do I believe them necessary to protect the wealthy; because enough of these will find their way into every branch of the legislation, to protect themselves. From fifteen to twenty legislatures of our own, in action for thirty years past, have proved that no fears of an equalization of property are to be apprehended from them. I think the best remedy is exactly that provided by all our constitutions, to leave to the citizens the free election and separation of the aristoi from the pseudo-aristoi, of the wheat from the chaff. In general they will elect the really good and wise. In some instances, wealth may corrupt, and birth blind them; but not in sufficient degree to endanger the society.

It is probable that our difference of opinion may, in some measure, be produced by a difference of character in those among whom we live. From what I have seen of Massachusetts and Connecticut myself, and still more from what I have heard, and the character given of the former by yourself, who know them so much better, there seems to be in those two States a traditionary reverence for certain families, which has rendered the offices of the government nearly hereditary in those families. I presume that from an early period of your history, members of those families happening to possess virtue and talents, have honestly exercised them for the good of the people, and by their services have endeared their names to them. . . . But although this hereditary succession to office with you, may, in some degree, be founded in real family merit, yet in a much higher degree, it has proceeded from your strict alliance of Church and State. These families are canonised in the eyes of the people on common principles, "you tickle me, and I will tickle you." In Virginia we have nothing of this. Our clergy, before the revolution, having been secured against rivalship by fixed salaries, did not give themselves the trouble of acquiring influence over the people. Of wealth, there were great accumulations in particular families, handed down from generation to generation, under the English law of entails. But the only object of ambition for the wealthy was a seat in the King's Council. All their court then was paid to the crown and its creatures; and they Philipised in all collisions between the King and the people. Hence they were unpopular; and that unpopularity continues attached to their names. A Randolph, a Carter, or a Burwell must have great personal superiority over a common competitor to be elected by the people even at this day. At the first session of our legislature after the Declaration of Independence, we passed a law abolishing entails. And this was followed by one abolishing the privilege of primogeniture, and dividing the lands of intestates equally among all their children, or other representatives. These laws, drawn by myself, laid the ax to the foot of pseudo-aristocracy. And had another which I prepared been adopted by the legislature, our work would have been complete. It was a bill for the more general diffusion of learning. This proposed to divide every county into wards of five or six miles square, like your townships; to establish in each ward a free school for reading, writing and common arithmetic; to provide for the annual selection of the best subjects from these schools, who might receive, at the public expense, a higher degree of education at a district school; and from these district schools to select a certain number of the most promising subjects to be completed at an University, where all the useful sciences should be taught. Worth and genius would thus have been sought out from every condition of life, and completely prepared by education for defeating the competition of wealth and birth for public trusts. My proposition had, for a further object, to impart to these wards those portions of self-government for which they are best qualified, by confiding to them the care of their poor, their roads, police, elections, the nomination of jurors, administration of justice in small cases, elementary exercises of militia; in short, to have made them little republics, with a warden at the head of each, for all those concerns which, being under their eye, they would better manage than the larger republics of the county or State. A general call of ward meetings by their wardens on the same day through the State, would at any time produce the genuine sense of the people on any required point, and would enable the State to act in mass, as your people have so often done, and with so much effect by their town meetings. The law for religious freedom, which made a part of this system, having put down the aristocracy of the clergy, and restored to the citizen the freedom of the mind, and those of entails and descents nurturing an equality of condition among them, this on education would have raised the mass of the people to the high ground of moral respectability necessary to their own safety, and to orderly government; and would have completed the great object of qualifying them to select the veritable aristoi, for the trusts of government, to the exclusion of the pseudalists ... Although this law has not yet been acted on but in a small and inefficient degree, it is still considered as before the legislature, with other bills of the revised code, not yet taken up, and I have great hope that some patriotic spirit will, at a favorable moment, call it up, and make it the key-stone of the arch of our government.

With respect to aristocracy, we should further consider, that before the establishment of the American States, nothing was known to history but the man of the old world, crowned within limits either small or overcharged, and steeped in the vices which that situation generates. A government adapted to such men would be one thing; but a very different one, that for the man of these States. Here every one may have land to labor for himself, if he chooses; or, preferring the exercise of any other industry, may exact for it such compensation as not only to afford a comfortable subsistence, but wherewith to provide for a cessation from labor in old age. Every one, by his property, or by his satisfactory situation, is interested in the support of law and order. And such men may safely and advantageously reserve to themselves a wholesome control over their public affairs, and a degree of freedom, which, in the hands of the *canaille* of the cities of Europe, would be instantly perverted to the demolition and destruction of everything public and private. The history of the last twenty-five years of France, and of the last forty years in America, nay of its last two hundred years, proves the truth of both parts of this observation.

But even in Europe a change has sensibly taken place in the mind of man. Science had liberated the ideas of those who read and reflect, and the American example had kindled feelings of right in the people. An insurrection has consequently begun, of science, talents, and courage, against rank and birth, which have fallen into contempt. It has failed in its first effort, because the mobs of the cities, the instrument used for its accomplishment, debased by ignorance, poverty and vice, could not be restrained to rational action. But the world will recover from the panic of this first catastrophe. Science is progressive, and talents and enterprise on the alert. Resort may be had to the people of the country, a more governable power from their principles and subordination; and rank, and birth, and tinsel-aristocracy will finally shrink into insignificance, even there. This, however, we have no right to meddle with. It suffices for us, if the moral and physical condition of our own citizens qualifies them to select the able and good for the direction of their government, with a recurrence of elections at such short periods as will enable them to displace an unfaithful servant, before the mischief he meditates may be irremediable.

I have thus stated my opinion on a point on which we differ, not with a view to controversy, for we are both too old to change opinions which are the result of a long life of inquiry and reflection; but on the suggestions of a former letter of yours, that we ought not to die before we have explained ourselves to each other. We acted in perfect harmony, through a long and perilous contest for our liberty and independence. A constitution has been acquired, which, though neither of us thinks perfect, yet both consider as competent to render our fellow citizens the happiest and the securest on whom the sun has ever shone. If we do not think exactly alike as to its imperfections, it matters little to our country, which, after devoting to it long lives of disinterested labor, we have delivered over to our successors in life, who will be able to take care of it and of themselves.

A Pluralist Solution

Robert A. Dahl

The Declaration of Independence contains these ringing phrases:

> That whenever any Form of Government becomes destructive of these ends, (Life, Liberty, and the pursuit of Happiness) it is the Right of the People to alter or to abolish it, and to institute a new Government, laying its foundation on such principles and organizing its powers in such form, as to them shall seem most likely to effect their Safety and Happiness.

Seventy years later, confronted by secession, and on the eve of war, in the inauguration speech . . . , Lincoln reaffirmed this principle:

> This country, with its institutions, belongs to the people who inhabit it. Whenever they shall grow weary of the existing government, they can exercise their constitutional right of amending it, or their revolutionary right to dismember or overthrow it.

But "the People" is an ambiguous phrase. Do these famous words mean that whenever a majority is discontented with the government it should be free to change it? If they are not permitted to do so, then can we say that they have given their approval, in any realistic sense, to the processes of government? Yet if every majority must be free to alter the rules of government, what is the significance of a "Constitution"? How can a constitution be more binding than ordinary law? Is there no legitimate way by which groups smaller than a majority can receive guarantees that the rules they agree to abide by will be more or less permanent and will not change at the whim of the next legislature?

These are difficult questions to answer, and no answers seem to command universal agreement. To gain "the consent of all" consistently applying the principle that the majority should be sovereign gives rise to serious problems, both logical and practical. Perhaps under certain unusual conditions, such as a very high degree of homogeneity, among a very small body of citizens, these problems could be solved.

In practise, however, popular governments have moved toward a rather different solution.

The practical solutions that democratic countries have evolved are a good deal less clear than a straightforward application of the principle of majority rule. These solutions seem less 'logical,' less coherent, more untidy, and a good deal more attainable. Patterns of democratic government do not reflect logically conceived philosophical plan so much as a series of responses to problems of diversity and conflict, by leaders who have sought to build and maintain a nation, to gain the loyalty and obedience of citizens, to win general and continuing approval of political institutions, and at the same time to conform to aspirations for democracy. However, some common elements can be discovered.

For one thing, in practise, countries with democratic regimes use force, just as other regimes do, to repel threats to the integrity of the national territory. Consequently secession is, as a practical matter, usually either impossible or extremely costly. (Colonies thought to lie outside the territory of the 'nation' may, of course, be granted independence.) To a considerable extent, then, large minorities are virtually 'compelled' to remain within the territorial limits of the nation. To make compulsory citizenship tolerable, great efforts are made to create and sustain a common sense of nationhood, so that minorities of all kinds will identify themselves with the nation. Hence secession or mass emigration are not usually thought of as practical alternatives.

Second, many matters of policy—religious beliefs and practises, for example—are effectively outside the legal authority of any government. Often they are placed beyond the legal authority of government through understandings and agreements widely shared and respected. In many cases these understandings and agreements are expressed in written constitutions that cannot be quickly or easily amended. Such a constitution is regarded as peculiarly binding; and ordinary laws that run counter to the constitution will be invalid, or, at the very least, subject to special scrutiny.

Third, a great many questions of policy are placed in the hands of private, semi-public, and local governmental organizations such as churches, families, business firms, trade unions, towns, cities, provinces, and the like. These questions of policy, like those left to individuals, are also effectively beyond the reach of national majorities, the national legislature, or indeed any national policy-makers acting in their legal and official capacities. In fact, whenever uniform policies are likely to be costly, difficult, or troublesome, in pluralistic democracies the tendency is to find ways by which these policies can be made by smaller groups of like-minded people who enjoy a high degree of legal independence.

Fourth, whenever a group of people believe that they are adversely affected by national policies or are about to be, they generally have extensive opportunities for presenting their case and for negotiations that may produce a more acceptable alternative. In some cases, they may have enough power to delay, to obstruct, and even to veto the attempt to impose policies on them.

Now in addition to all these characteristics, the United States has limited the sovereignty of the majority in still other ways. In fact, the United

States has gone so far in this direction that it is sometimes called a pluralistic system, a term I propose to use here.

The fundamental axiom in the theory and practise of American pluralism is, I believe, this: Instead of a single center of sovereign power there must be multiple centers of power, none of which is or can be wholly sovereign. Although the only legitimate sovereign is the people, in the perspective of American pluralism even the people ought never to be an absolute sovereign; consequently no part of the people, such as a majority, ought to be absolutely sovereign.

Why this axiom? The theory and practise of American pluralism tend to assume, as I see it, that the existence of multiple centers of power, none of which is wholly sovereign, will help (may indeed be necessary) to tame power, to secure the consent of all, and to settle conflicts peacefully:

> Because one center of power is set against another, power itself will be tamed, civilized, controlled, and limited to decent human purposes, while coercion, the most evil form of power, will be reduced to a minimum.
>
> Because even minorities are provided with opportunities to veto solutions they strongly object to, the consent of all will be won in the long run.
>
> Because constant negotiations among different centers of power are necessary in order to make decisions, citizens and leaders will perfect the precious art of dealing peacefully with their conflicts, and not merely to the benefit of one partisan but to the mutual benefit of all the parties to a conflict.

These are, I think, the basic postulates and even the unconscious ways of thought that are central to the American attempt to cope with the inescapable problems of power, conflict, and consent.

Elitism In a Democracy

Peter Bachrach

The tension between liberalism and democracy—between freedom to be left alone and freedom to participate in decisions which affect oneself and one's community—is evident among contemporary liberals. Until recently the works of de Tocqueville were regarded as historically "dated." Today his thesis on the perverse impact of equalitarianism upon a free society is seriously studied by all students of democracy.

In the past, the democratic theorists experienced little difficulty in reconciling democracy and liberalism. For in the eighteenth and nineteenth centuries, the threat of tyranny emanated primarily from the ruling elites, from corrupt and decadent monarchies, and from power-hungry, arbitrary, and unrepresentative parliaments. Jefferson's support for a constitutional system of checks and balances was not prompted, as it was in the *Federalist Papers*, by fear of majority tyranny of the people, but by fear of minority tyranny of the ruling elite. For the same reason, he insisted upon a Bill of Rights, not as a shield against majority tyranny, but to protect the principle of majority rule. To be sure, people were corruptible, but it was assumed that the source of corruption was faulty political, economic, and social institutions.

To free man from the corrupting forces of society was imperative if the majority was to fulfill its responsibility of performing the task as guardian of society's freedom. Thus what was called for was more, not less, democracy. This entailed not only extending the right of the franchise, but also, as neo-liberals such as Hobhouse were later to advocate, utilizing government to provide a minimum standard of living for all and the protection of the individual from the arbitrary wielding of power by nongovernmental groups and organizations.

In the course of the evolution of democratic government during the nineteenth century and the first thirty-five years of the twentieth, democrats generally believed that the continued extension and growth of democracy was the best assurance of the preservation of constitutional liberalism. From the outset, the belief was grounded on the assumption that the common man inherently was capable of good judgment and that his occasional manifestations of irrationality and hostility toward the democratic process were symptomatic of a malfunctioning society.

Events reaffirmed the faith of the liberal democrat. Especially in England and America, it was the great mass of people, first the middle and then the working classes, who were the major force in extending democracy and constitutional liberties. In exerting continuous pressure for the expansion of the franchise, they were instrumental in building the foundations of modern democratic constitutionalism—the two party system. And if the working classes had not waged a long and bitter struggle for essential economic and social reform, it is doubtful that even a remnant of constitutionalism would have survived in the world today. Freedom of speech, crucial as an instrument of majorities in their struggle for reform, appeared not only to safeguard civil liberties but to broaden and vitalize them. Moreover, it appeared equally true that Jefferson was basically right: that in the last analysis, it is the mass of the people, not the elite, who are the true guardians of liberty.

Even the rise of totalitarianism in Italy and Germany, and the stark realization of its existence in the Soviet Union, did not noticeably dampen democratic beliefs. In fact, it made some democrats more militant. For example, on the eve of World War II, Carl Becker argued that the proper and effective retort to fascist and Communist challenge was widespread internal economic and social reform. He was convinced that the survival of democracy depended upon the rectification of the "flagrant inequality of possessions and of opportunity now existing in democratic societies." Not to adopt effective means to achieve this objective, he observed, would be to invite the common man to turn to another system which promised a tolerable life. Becker, who was the epitome of Aristotle's moderate man, could see no effective means for safeguarding the democratic process other than to democratize society at least to the point where all groups within its bounds could reasonably be expected to be attached to it. Also adhering to this thesis, Max Lerner argued that the Weimar Republic fell not because of an overzealous majority but because of political stalemate, the inability of the government to act decisively in the interests of the majority of the people. He recognized the dangers inherent in majority rule, but he regarded the irresponsible actions of elites upon the body politic as a greater danger. He called for the rise of a militant democracy to reassert itself against the "aristocracy of wealth and the insolence of power." Like Becker he saw no way to safeguard civil liberties other than by effectively organizing majority will in support of vigorous and dynamic government. "I can say only that the political job of our time must be the heroic effect of making our society as safe as possible for the majority principle."

With the onslaught of postwar reaction and the rise of McCarthyism in America, the democratic faith in the common man, if not shattered, was subjected to serious doubt. The widespread alliance between workingmen and the Communist parties in France and Italy, and trade union support of Perón in Argentina and Salazar in Portugal could be discounted to an extent in terms of Becker's and Lerner's thesis, but the persistent threat to freedom from these quarters was a new and frightening phenomenon. For unlike the days of the Alien and Sedition Acts and the Palmer raids, McCarthy was not vigorously opposed by any sector in the society and had the tacit approval, if not the active support, of an uncomfortably large number of people from all strata of society. What was particularly baffling was that the McCarthyite reaction occurred and persisted during a period of relative affluence. On hindsight, it appears that affluence is conducive to reaction for two reasons: first, it is an ideal setting for those suffering from the social tensions of an acquisitive society to vent their anxieties and bewilderment in political movements of the right. Secondly, it tends to dry up political protest from the left; the labor movement becomes nonmilitant and businesslike; intellectuals situated in lucrative and prestigious posts lose their taste for social criticism.

Such an explanation, however, does not, in the eyes of either liberal or radical democrats, alter their disillusionment about the common man. He turns out, after all, not to be attached to the cause of liberty, fraternity, or, indeed, equality; and when his socioeconomic interests are not at stake, he may become indifferent toward the fate of freedom itself. It is feared that, given the opportunity, he is more inclined to support than oppose the demagogue's attack against freedom.

This is the chief reason, I suggest, for the radical shift in democratic thought in the postwar period. The nature of this shift is illustrated most clearly in Max Lerner's writings. For example, in his ambitious book, *America as Civilization* (1957), Lerner seems more concerned with defending than with reforming the American political system; the dangers of political stalemate and of minority rule are pushed aside in favor of praise for the "widespread diffusion of power and the talent for equilibrium [that the American system] has shown." A similar shift, although considerably less marked, is also reflected in the writings of Franz Neuman during the last few years of his life. He too retreated from pressing for a further democratization of society to a defense of existing democratic systems. And to defend the system, he did not turn to the proletarian but "to the scholars, teachers, intellectuals and artists." Liberals generally became disinclined toward the traditional criticism of American institutions voiced by Parrington, Beard, and J. Allen Smith, and began to emphasize the dangers of majority tyranny and extol the virtues of judicial review, checks and balances, and the pluralist system, characterized by compromise and government by consensus. The authority of social science has in recent years increasingly supported this position.

The findings of public opinion and personality research documented the theorists' suspicion that the great majority of people have a surprisingly weak commitment to democratic values. Samuel Stouffer's study on the attitude of Americans toward civil liberties showed that the rank and file of organizations are less attached than leaders to the principles of civil liberties and democratic procedures. Moreover, his study showed that leaders from conservative organizations, such as the Daughters of the American Revolution, were more permissive toward the rights of others than the rank and file of liberal organizations, such as trade unions. In his article "Working Class Authoritarianism," Seymour Lipset reached the conclusion, based upon findings of numerous studies, that the lower strata are relatively more authoritarian than either the middle or upper classes. The authoritarian predispositions of the lower classes, he believes, are caused chiefly by social isolation and lack of sufficient exposure to and participation in either political or voluntary organizations. Lipset cautions the reader, however, that the latent authoritarianism of the working classes does not necessarily constitute a threat to the democratic system. A combination of factors would have to exist for this force to become overt. Nevertheless, the major thrust of his argument is that, all other things being equal, the working classes are the major threat to freedom.

With the disenchantment with the common man, the classical view of the elite-mass relationship has become reversed: it is the common man, not the elite, who is chiefly suspected of endangering freedom, and it is the elite, not the common man, who is looked upon as the chief guardian of the system. The revolt from the masses has led to a second shift in theory: the emphasis is no longer upon extending or strengthening democracy, but upon stabilizing the established system. The focus, in short, is upon protecting liberalism from the excesses of democracy rather than upon utilizing liberal means to progress toward the realization of democratic ideals. Political equilibrium is the fundamental value of the new theory. Thus the political passivity of the great majority of the people is not regarded as an element of democratic malfunctioning, but on the contrary, as a necessary condition for allowing the creative functioning of the elite. The empirical and normative aspects of the theory supplement each other: empirically we find that the masses are relatively unreliable but as a rule passive, and the elites relatively reliable and dominant in making the important decisions for society. The on-going system tends to be the desired system.

These observations, I believe, are well reflected in the currently developing theory of democratic elitism.

David Truman, *The Governmental Process* (New York: Knopf, 1951). The most enduring statement of the theory that power in society is divided among a variety of competing groups. A landmark in pluralist literature.

Peter Bachrach and Morton Baratz, "Decisions and Nondecisions: An Analytical Framework," *American Political Science Review,* LVII (1963), pp. 632-642. The essential argument is that elites should be evaluated not only for their influence in decision-making situations, but also for their ability to prevent certain issues from reaching the decision-making stage.

Richard Merelman, "On the Neo-Elitist Critique of Community Power," *American Political Science Review,* LXII (June, 1968), pp. 451-460. A direct assault upon the neo-elitists, and a restatement of pluralist arguments.

Jack Walker, "A Critique of the Elitist Theory of Democracy," *American Political Science Review,* LX (June, 1966), pp. 255-295. A major essay challenging pluralism theoretically, empirically, and normatively.

3

The American
Constitution: Protecting
"Principle and
Property"

Contrary to the statement in its preamble, the Constitution of the United States was *not* "ordained and established" by "the people." It was written by a small, educated, talented, wealthy elite in America who represented powerful economic interests: bond holders, investors, merchants, real estate owners, and planters.

An elitist interpretation of the Constitution, and the basic structure of American government, emphasizes the following:

(1) The Constitution was not written by "the people" but by a small unrepresentative elite in the new nation. The vast majority of Americans did not participate either directly or indirectly in the establishment of the United States government.

(2) The Constitution and our national government had its origins in elite dissatisfaction with the inability of the central government to pay off its bond holders, the interference of state governments with the development of a national economy, the threat of cheap paper money, laws relieving debtors of their obligations, the threat of post-revolutionary war radicalism, and the lack of any army capable of protecting western land, or any navy capable of protecting maritime commercial interests.

(3) This same elite shared a consensus that the purpose of government was the protection of liberty and property. They believed in government by men of principal and property and they opposed mass democracy and direct popular participation in decision-making. They feared mass movements that would seek to reduce inequalities of wealth.

(4) The structure of the American government was designed to suppress "factious" issues, or threats to dominant economic elites. Republicanism, the division of power between state and national government, and the complex system of checks and balances and divided power, were all designed as buffers against mass movements which threatened liberty and property.

(5) While all Americans may have benefited from the adoption of the Constitution, it was the direct and immediate benefit in that document for America's elites which provided the impelling motive for its creation.

The *Federalist Papers* are the most important interpretive documents of this early period in American political history. They were written by Alexander Hamilton, James Madison, and John Jay during the debates over the adoption of the Constitution, and they explain and defend that Constitution and the government which it was to establish. In what has become the most famous essay of the Federalist Papers, James Madison argues that *controlling factions* is "the principle task of modern legislation." He admits that factions can arise for many reasons but "the most common and durable source of factions has been the various and unequal distribution of property." In Madison's view, the fundamental problem in constructing the national government was the protection of property against mass movements. The structure of the new national government was deliberately designed to ensure the suppression of "factious" issues; and Madison does not hedge in naming these issues: "a rage for paper money, an abolition of debts, equal division of property, or any other improper or wicked project. . . ." All these issues were challenges to the dominant economic elites. Madison defended the new Constitution because its Republican and federal features would help keep certain threats to property from ever becoming public issues.

The foremost historian of the American Constitution, Charles Beard, has described "the underlying political science of the Constitution," and the economic interests which were the direct and immediate beneficiaries of its various provisions. His *An Economic Interpretation of the Constitution* is the most important and controversial study of the Constitution to date. Beard's thesis about class conflict over the adoption of the Constitution is a controversial one among historians, but there is little doubt that he accurately describes the advantages which America's economic elites derived from the adoption of the Constitution and the establishment of the new government.

Historian Richard Hofstadter contends in our third selection, *The American Political Tradition,* that the Founding Fathers had no intention of turning government over to people who "have ever been and ever will be unfit to retain the exercise of power in their own hands." While he feels it is true that the Founding Fathers believed in republicanism—that is, that they believed that legitimate government rested upon the consent of the governed—they nonetheless also considered the masses clearly unfit to govern themselves. Government, thought the Fathers, should be run by men of principle and property.

Controlling Factions

James Madison

To the People of the State of New York:

Among the numerous advantages promised by a well-constructed Union, none deserves to be more accurately developed than its tendency to break and control the violence of faction. The friend of popular governments never finds himself so much alarmed for their character and fate, as when he contemplates their propensity to this dangerous vice. He will not fail, therefore, to set a due value on any plan which, without violating the principles to which he is attached, provides a proper cure for it. The instability, injustice, and confusion introduced into the public councils, have, in truth, been the mortal diseases under which popular governments have everywhere perished; as they continue to be the favorite and fruitful topics from which the adversaries to liberty derive their most specious declamations. The valuable improvements made by the American constitutions on the popular models, both ancient and modern, cannot certainly be too much admired; but it would be an unwarrantable partiality, to contend that they have as effectually obviated the danger on this side, as was wished and expected. Complaints are everywhere heard from our most considerate and virtuous citizens, equally the friends of public and private faith, and of public and personal liberty, that our governments are too unstable, that the public good is disregarded in the conflicts of rival parties, and that measures are too often decided, not according to the rules of justice and the rights of the minor party, but by the superior force of an interested and overbearing majority. However anxiously we may wish that these complaints had no foundation, the evidence of known facts will not permit us to deny that they are in some degree true. It will be found, indeed, on a candid review of our situation, that some of the distresses under which we labor have been erroneously charged on the operation of our governments; but it will be found, at the same time, that other causes will not alone account for many of our heaviest misfortunes; and, particularly, for that prevailing and increasing distrust of public engagements, and alarm for private rights, which are echoed from one end of the continent to the other. These must be chiefly, if not wholly, effects of the unsteadiness and injustice with which a factious spirit has tainted our public administrations.

By a faction, I understand a number of citizens, whether amounting to a majority or minority of the whole, who are united and actuated by some common impulse of passion, or of interest, adverse to the rights of other citizens, or to the permanent and aggregate interests of the community.

There are two methods of curing the mischiefs of faction: the one, by removing its causes; the other, by controlling its effects.

There are again two methods of removing the causes of faction: the one, by destroying the liberty which is essential to its existence; the other, by giving to every citizen the same opinions, the same passions, and the same interests.

It could never be more truly said than of the first remedy, that it was worse than the disease. Liberty is to faction what air is to fire, an ailment without which it instantly expires. But it could not be less folly to abolish liberty, which is essential to political life, because it nourishes faction, than it would be to wish the annihilation of air, which is essential to animal life, because it imparts to fire its destructive agency.

The second expedient is as impracticable as the first would be unwise. As long as the reason of man continues fallible, and he is at liberty to exercise it, different opinions will be formed. As long as the connection subsists between his reason and his self-love, his opinions and his passions will have a reciprocal influence on each other; and the former will be objects to which the latter will attach themselves. The diversity in the faculties of men, from which the rights of property originate, is not less an insuperable obstacle to a uniformity of interests. The protection of these faculties is the first object of government. From the protection of different and unequal faculties of acquiring property, the possession of different degrees and kinds of property immediately results; and from the influence of these on the sentiments and views of the respective proprietors, ensues a division of the society into different interests and parties.

The latent causes of faction are thus sown in the nature of man; and we see them everywhere brought into different degrees of activity, according to the different circumstances of civil society. A zeal for different opinions concerning religion, concerning government, and many other points, as well of speculation as of practice; an attachment to different leaders ambitiously contending for pre-eminence and power; or to persons of other descriptions whose fortunes have been interesting to the human passions, have, in turn, divided mankind into parties, inflamed them with mutual animosity, and rendered them much more disposed to vex and oppress each other than to co-operate for their common good. So strong is this propensity of mankind to fall into mutual animosities, that where no substantial occasion presents itself, the most frivolous and fanciful distinctions have been sufficient to kindle their unfriendly passions and excite their most violent conflicts. But the most common and durable source of factions has been the various and unequal distribution of property. Those who hold and those who are without property have ever formed distinct interests in society. Those who are creditors, and those who are debtors, fall under a like discrimination. A landed interest, a manufacturing interest, a mercantile interest, a moneyed interest, with many lesser interests, grow up of necessity in civilized nations, and divide them into different classes, actuated by different sentiments and views. The regulation of these various and interfering interests forms the principal task of modern legislation, and involves the spirit of party and faction in the necessary and ordinary operations of the government.

No man is allowed to be a judge in his own cause, because his interest would certainly bias his judgment, and, not improbably, corrupt his integrity. With equal, nay with greater reason, a body of men are unfit to be both judges and parties at the same time; yet what are many of the most important acts of legislation, but so many judicial determinations, not indeed concerning the rights of large bodies of citizens? And what are the different classes of legislators but advocates and parties to the causes which they determine? Is a law proposed concerning private debts? It is a question to which the creditors are parties on one side and the debtors on the other. Justice ought to hold the balance between them. Yet the parties are, and must be, themselves the judges; and the most numerous party, or, in other words, the most powerful faction must be expected to prevail. Shall domestic manufactures be encouraged, and in what degree, by restrictions on foreign manufactures? are questions which would be differently decided by the landed and the manufacturing classes, and probably by neither with a sole regard to justice and the public good. The apportionment of taxes on the various descriptions of property is an act which seems to require the most exact impartiality; yet there is, perhaps, no legislative act in which greater opportunity and temptation are given to a predominant party to trample on the rules of justice. Every shilling with which they overburden the inferior number, is a shilling saved to their own pockets.

It is in vain to say that enlightened statesmen will be able to adjust these clashing interests, and render them all subservient to the public good. Enlightened statesmen will not always be at the helm. Nor, in many cases, can such an adjustment be made at all without taking into view indirect and remote considerations, which will rarely prevail over the immediate interest which one party may find in disregarding the rights of another or the good of the whole.

The inference to which we are brought is, that the *causes* of faction cannot be removed, and that relief is only to be sought in the means of controlling its *effects*.

If a faction consists of less than a majority, relief is supplied by the republican principle, which enables the majority to defeat its sinister views by regular vote. It may clog the administration, it may convulse the society; but it will be unable to execute and mask its violence under the forms of the Constitution. When a majority is included in a faction, the form of popular government, on the other hand, enables it to sacrifice to its ruling passion or interest both the public good and the rights of other citizens. To secure the public good and private rights against the danger of such a faction, and at the same time to preserve the spirit and the form of popular government, is then the great object to which our inquiries are directed. Let me add that it is the desideratum by which this form of government can be rescued from the opprobrium under which it has so long labored, and be recommended to the esteem and adoption of mankind.

By what means is this object attainable? Evidently by one of two only. Either the existence of the same passion or interest in a majority at the same time must be prevented, or the majority, having such coexistent passion or interest, must be rendered, by their number and local situation, unable to concert and carry into effect schemes of oppression. If the impulse and the opportunity be suffered to coincide, we well know that neither moral nor religious motives can be relied on as an adequate control. They are not found to be such on the injustice and violence of individuals, and lose their efficacy in proportion to the number combined together, that is, in proportion as their efficacy becomes needful.

From this view of the subject it may be concluded that a pure democracy, by which I mean a society consisting of a small number of citizens, who assemble and administer the government in person, can admit of no cure for the mischiefs of faction. A common passion or interest will, in almost every case, be felt by a majority of the whole; a communication and concert result from the form of government itself; and there is nothing to check the inducements to sacrifice the weaker party or an obnoxious individual. Hence it is that such democracies have ever been spectacles of turbulence and contention; have ever been found incompatible with personal security or the rights of property; and have in general been as short in their lives as they have been violent in their deaths. Theoretic politicians, who have patronized this species of government, have erroneously supposed that by reducing mankind to a perfect equality in their political rights, they would, at the same time, be perfectly equalized and assimilated in their possessions, their opinions, and their passions.

A republic, by which I mean a government in which the scheme of representation takes place, opens a different prospect, and promises the cure for which we are seeking. Let us examine the points in which it varies from pure democracy, and we shall comprehend both the nature of the cure and the efficacy which it must derive from the Union.

The two great points of difference between a democracy and a republic are: first, the delegation of the government, in the latter, to a small number of citizens elected by the rest; secondly, the greater number of citizens, and greater sphere of country, over which the latter may be extended.

The effect of the first difference is, on the one hand, to refine and enlarge the public views, by passing them through the medium of a chosen body of citizens, whose wisdom may best discern the true interest of their country, and whose patriotism and love of justice will be least likely to sacrifice it to temporary or partial considerations. Under such a regulation, it may well happen that the public voice, pronounced by the representatives of the people, will be more consonant to the public good than if pronounced by the people themselves, convened for the purpose. On the other hand, the effect may be inverted. Men of factious tempers, of local prejudices, or of sinister designs, may, by intrigue, by corruption, or by other means, first obtain the suffrages, and then betray the interests, of the people. The question resulting is, whether small or extensive republics are more favorable to the election of proper guardians of the public weal; and it is clearly decided in favor of the latter by two obvious considerations:

In the first place, it is to be remarked that, however small the republic may be, the representatives must be raised to a certain number, in order to guard against the cabals of a few; and that, however large it may be, they must be limited to a certain number, in order to guard against the confusion of a multitude. Hence, the number of representatives in the two cases not being in proportion to that of the two constituents, and being proportionally greater in the small republic, it follows that, if the proportion of fit characters be not less in the large than in the small republic, the former will present a greater option, and consequently a greater probability of a fit choice.

In the next place, as each representative will be chosen by a greater number of citizens in the large than in the small republic, it will be more difficult for unworthy candidates to practise with success the vicious arts by which elections are too often carried; and the suffrages of the people being more free, will be more likely to centre in men who possess the most attractive merit and the most diffusive and established characters.

It must be confessed that in this, as in most other cases, there is a mean, on both sides of which inconveniences will be found to lie. By enlarging too much the number of electors, you render the representative too little acquainted with all their local circumstances and lesser interests; as by reducing it too much, you render him unduly attached to these, and too little fit to comprehend and pursue great and national objects. The federal Constitution forms a happy combination in this respect; the great and aggregate interests being referred to the national, the local and particular to the State legislatures.

The other point of difference is, the greater number of citizens and extent of territory which may be brought within the compass of republican than of democratic government; and it is this circumstance principally which renders factious combinations less to be dreaded in the former than in the latter. The smaller the society, the fewer probably will be the distinct parties and interests composing it; the fewer the distinct parties and interests, the more frequently will a majority be found of the same party; and the smaller the number of individuals composing a majority, and the smaller the compass within which they are placed, the more easily will they concert and execute their plans of oppression. Extend the sphere and you take in a greater variety of parties and interests; you make it less probable that a majority of the whole will have a common motive to invade the rights of other citizens; or if such a common motive exists, it will be more difficult for all who feel it to discover their own strength, and to act in unison with each other. Besides other impediments, it may be remarked that, where there is a consciousness of unjust or dishonorable purposes, communication is always checked by distrust in proportion to the number whose concurrence is necessary.

Hence, it clearly appears, that the same advantage which a republic has over a democracy, in controlling the effects of faction, is enjoyed by a large over a small republic,—is enjoyed by the Union over the States composing it. Does the advantage consist in the substitution of representatives whose enlightened views and virtuous sentiments render them superior to local prejudices and to schemes of injustice? It will not be denied that the representation of the Union will be most likely to possess these requisite endowments. Does it consist in the greater security afforded by a greater variety of parties, against the event of any one party being able to outnumber and oppress the rest? In an equal degree does the increased variety of parties comprised within the Union, increase this security. Does it, in fine, consist in the greater obstacles opposed to the concert and accomplishment of the secret wishes of an unjust and interested majority? Here, again, the extent of the Union gives it the most palpable advantage.

The influence of factious leaders may kindle a flame within their particular States, but will be unable to spread a general conflagration through the other States. A religious sect may degenerate into a political faction in a part of the Confederacy; but the variety of sects dispersed over the entire face of it must secure the national councils against any danger from that source. A rage for paper money, for an abolition of debts, for an equal division of property, or for any other improper or wicked project, will be less apt to pervade the whole body of the Union than a particular member of it; in the same proportion as such a malady is more likely to taint a particular county or district, than an entire State.

In the extent and proper structure of the Union, therefore, we behold a republican remedy for the diseases most incident to republican government. And according to the degree of pleasure and pride we feel in being republicans, ought to be our zeal in cherishing the spirit and supporting the character of Federalists.

Publius

The Constitution as an Economic Document

Charles Beard

It is difficult for the superficial student of the Constitution, who has read only the commentaries of the legists, to conceive of that instrument as an economic document. It places no property qualifications on voters or officers; it gives no outward recognition of any economic groups in society; it mentions no special privileges to be conferred upon any class. It betrays no feeling, such as vibrates through the French constitution of 1791; its language is cold, formal, and severe.

The true inwardness of the Constitution is not revealed by an examination of its provisions as simple propositions of law; but by a long and careful study of the voluminous correspondence of the period, contemporary newspapers and pamphlets, the records of the debates in the Convention at Philadelphia and in the several state conventions, and particularly, *The Federalist,* which was widely circulated during the struggle over ratification. The correspondence shows the exact character of the evils which the Constitution was intended to remedy; the records of the proceedings in the Philadelphia Convention reveal the successive steps in the building of the framework of the government under the pressure of economic interests; the pamphlets and newspapers disclose the ideas of the contestants over the ratification; and *The Federalist* presents the political science of the new system as conceived by three of the profoundest thinkers of the period, Hamilton, Madison, and Jay.

Doubtless, the most illuminating of these sources on the economic character of the Constitution are the records of the debates in the Convention, which have come down to us in fragmentary form; and a thorough treatment of material forces reflected in the several clauses of the instrument of government created by the grave assembly at Philadelphia would require a rewriting of the history of the proceedings in the light of the great interests represented there. But an entire volume would scarcely suffice to present the results of such a survey, and an undertaking of this character is accordingly impossible here.

The Federalist, on the other hand, presents in a relatively brief and systematic form an economic interpretation of the Constitution by the men best fitted, through an intimate knowledge of the ideals of the framers, to expound the political science of the new government. This wonderful piece of argumentation by Hamilton, Madison, and Jay is in fact the finest study in the economic interpretation of politics which exists in any language; and whoever would understand the Constitution as a economic document need hardly go beyond it. It is true that the tone of the writers is somewhat modified on account of the fact that they are appealing to the voters to ratify the Constitution, but at the same time they are, by the force of circumstances, compelled to convince large economic groups that safety and strength lie in the adoption of the new system.

Indeed, every fundamental appeal in it is to some material and substantial interest. Sometimes it is to the people at large in the name of protection against invading armies and European coalitions. Sometimes it is to the commercial classes whose business is represented as prostrate before the follies of the Confederation. Now it is to creditors seeking relief against paper money and the assaults of the agrarians in general; now it is to the holders of federal securities which are depreciating toward the vanishing point. But above all, it is to the owners of personalty anxious to find a foil against the attacks of levelling democracy, that the authors of *The Federalist* address their most cogent arguments in favor of ratification. It is true there is much discussion of the details of the new frame-work of government, to which even some friends of reform took exceptions; but Madison and Hamilton both knew that these were incidental matters when compared with the sound basis upon which the superstructure rested.

In reading the pages of this remarkable work as a study in political economy, it is important to bear in mind that the system, which the authors are describing, consisted of two fundamental parts—one positive, the other negative:

(1) A government endowed with certain positive powers, but so constructed as to break the force of majority rule and prevent invasions of the property rights of minorities.
(2) Restrictions on the state legislatures which had been so vigorous in their attacks on capital.

Under some circumstances, action is the immediate interest of the dominant party; and whenever it desires to make an economic gain through governmental functioning, it must have, of course, a system endowed with the requisite powers.

Examples of this are to be found in protective tariffs, in ship subsidies, in railway land grants, in river and harbor improvements, and so on through the catalogue of so-called "paternalistic" legislation. Of course it may be shown that the "general good" is the ostensible object of any particular act; but the general good is a passive force, and unless we know who are the several individuals that benefit in its name, it has no meaning. When it is so analyzed, immediate and remote beneficiaries are discovered; and the former are usually found to have been the dynamic element in securing the legislation. Take for example, the economic interests of the advocates who appear in tariff hearings at Washington.

On the obverse side, dominant interests quite as often benefit from the prevention of governmental action as from positive assistance. They are able to take care of themselves if let alone within the circle of protection created by the law. Indeed, most owners of property have as much to fear from positive governmental action as from their inability to secure advantageous legislation. Particularly is this true where the field of private property is already extended to cover practically every form of tangible and intangible wealth. This was clearly set forth by Hamilton: "It may perhaps be said that the power of preventing bad laws includes that of preventing good ones. . . . But this objection will have little weight with those who can properly estimate the mischiefs of that inconstancy and mutability in the laws which form the greatest blemish in the character and genius of our governments. They will consider every institution calculated to restrain the excess of law-making, and to keep things in the same state in which they happen to be at any given period, as more likely to do good than harm. . . . The injury which may possibly be done by defeating a few good laws will be amply compensated by the advantage of preventing a number of bad ones."

The Underlying Political Science of the Constitution

Before taking up the economic implications of the structure of the federal government, it is important to ascertain what, in the opinion of *The Federalist*, is the basis of all government. The most philosophical examination of the foundations of political science is made by Madison in the tenth number. Here he lays down, in no uncertain language, the principle that the first and elemental concern of every government is economic.

(1) "The first object of government," he declares, is the protection of "the diversity in the faculties of men, from which the rights of property originate." The chief business of government, from which, perforce, its essential nature must be derived, consists in the control and adjustment of conflicting economic interests. After enumerating the various forms of propertied interests which spring up inevitably in modern society, he adds: "The regulation of these various and interfering interests forms the principal task of modern legislation, and involves the spirit of party and faction in the ordinary operations of the government."

(2) What are the chief causes of these conflicting political forces with which the government must concern itself? Madison answers. Of course fanciful and frivolous distinctions have sometimes been the cause of violent conflicts; "but the most common and durable source of factions has been the various and unequal distribution of property. Those who hold and those who are without property have ever formed distinct interests in society. Those who are creditors, and those who are debtors, fall under a like discrimination. A landed interest, a manufacturing interest, a mercantile interest, a moneyed interest, with many lesser interests grow up of necessity in civilized nations, and divide them into different classes actuated by different sentiments and views."

(3) The theories of government which men entertain are emotional reactions to their property interests. "From the protection of different and unequal faculties of acquiring property, the possession of different degrees and kinds of property immediately results; *and from the influence of these on the sentiments and views of the respective proprietors, ensues a division of society into different interests and parties.*" Legislatures reflect these interests. "What," he asks, "are

the different classes of legislators but advocates and parties to the causes which they determine." There is no help for it. "The causes of faction cannot be removed," and "we well know that neither moral nor religious motives can be relied on as an adequate control."

(4) Unequal distribution of property is inevitable, and from it contending factions will rise in the state. The government will reflect them, for they will have their separate principles and "sentiments"; but the supreme danger will arise from the fusion of certain interests into an overbearing majority, which Madison, in another place, prophesied would be the landless proletariat,—an overbearing majority which will make its "rights" paramount, and sacrifice the "rights" of the minority. "To secure the public good," he declares, "and private rights against the danger of such a faction and at the same time preserve the spirit and the form of popular government is then the great object to which our inquiries are directed."

(5) How is this to be done? Since the contending classes cannot be eliminated and their interests are bound to be reflected in politics, the only way out lies in making it difficult for enough contending interests to fuse into a majority, and in balancing one over against another. The machinery for doing this is created by the new Constitution and by the Union. (a) Public views are to be refined and enlarged "by passing them through the medium of a chosen body of citizens." (b) The very size of the Union will enable the inclusion of more interests so that the danger of an overbearing majority is not so great. "The smaller the society, the fewer probably will be the distinct parties and interests, composing it; the fewer the distinct parties and interests, the more frequently will a majority be found of the same party. . . . Extend the sphere, and you take in a greater variety of parties and interests; you make it less probably that a majority of the whole will have a common motive to invade the rights of other citizens; or if such a common motive exists, it will be more difficult for all who feel it to discover their strength and to act in unison with each other."

Q.E.D., "in the extent and proper structure of the Union, therefore, we behold a republican remedy for the diseases most incident to republican government."

The Structure of Government or the Balance of Powers

The fundamental theory of political economy thus stated by Madison was the basis of the original American conception of the balance of powers which is formulated at length in four numbers of *The Federalist* and consists of the following elements:

(1) No mere parchment separation of departments of government will be effective. "The legislative department is everywhere extending the sphere of its activity, and drawing all power into its impetuous vortex. The founders of our republic . . . seem never for a moment to have turned their eyes from the danger to liberty from the overgrown and all-grasping prerogative of an hereditary magistrate, supported and fortified by an hereditary branch of the legislative

authority. They seem never to have recollected the danger from legislative usurpations, which, by assembling all power in the same hands, must lead to the same tyranny as is threatened by executive usurpations."

(2) Some sure mode of checking usurpations in the government must be provided, other than frequent appeals to the people. "There appear to be insuperable objections against the proposed recurrence to the people as a provision in all cases for keeping the several departments of power within their constitutional limits." In a contest between the legislature and the other branches of the government, the former would doubtless be victorious on account of the ability of the legislators to plead their cause with the people.

(3) What then can be depended upon to keep the government in close rein? "The only answer that can be given is, that as all these exterior provisions are found to be inadequate, the defect must be supplied by so contriving the interior structure of the government as that its several constituent parts may, by their mutual relations, be the means of keeping each other in their proper places. . . . It is of great importance in a republic not only to guard the society against the oppression of its rulers, but to guard one part of the society against the injustice of the other part. Different interests necessarily exist in different classes of citizens. If a majority be united by a common interest, the rights of the minority will be insecure." There are two ways of obviating this danger: one is by establishing a monarch independent of popular will, and the other is by reflecting these contending interests (so far as their representatives may be enfranchised) in the very structure of the government itself so that a majority cannot dominate the minority—which minority is of course composed of those who possess property that may be attacked. "Society itself will be broken into so many parts, interests, and classes of citizens, that the rights of individuals, or of the minority, will be in little danger from interested combinations of the majority."

(4) The structure of the government as devised at Philadelphia reflects these several interests and makes improbable any danger to the minority from the majority. "The House of Representatives being to be elected immediately by the people, the Senate by the State legislatures, the President by electors chosen for that purpose by the people, there would be little probability of a common interest to cement these different branches in a predilection for any particular class of electors."

(5) All of these diverse interests appear in the amending process but they are further reinforced against majorities. An amendment must receive a two-thirds vote in each of the two houses so constituted and the approval of three-fourths of the states.

(6) The economic corollary of this system is as follows: Property interests may, through their superior weight in power and intelligence, secure advantageous legislation whenever necessary, and they may at the same time obtain immunity from control by parliamentary majorities.

If we examine carefully the delicate instrument by which the framers sought to check certain kinds of positive action that might be advocated to the detriment of established and acquired rights, we cannot help marvelling at their skill. Their leading idea was to break up the attacking forces at the starting point: the source of political authority for the several branches of the government. This disintegration of positive action at the source was further facilitated by the differentiation in the terms given to the respective departments of the government. And the crowning counterweight to "an interested and over-bearing majority," as Madison phrased it, was secured in the peculiar position assigned to the judiciary, and the use of the sanctity and mystery of the law as a foil to democratic attacks. . . .

The motion to strike out the "landed" qualification for legislators was carried by a vote of ten to one; the proposition to strike out the disqualification of persons having unsettled accounts with the United States was carried by a vote of nine to two. Finally the proposition to exclude persons who were indebted to the United States was likewise defeated by a vote of nine to two, after Pinckney had called attention to the fact that "it would exclude persons who had purchased confiscated property or should purchase Western territory of the public and might be some obstacle to the sale of the latter."

Indeed, there was little risk to personalty in thus allowing the Constitution to go to the states for approval without any property qualifications on voters other than those which the state might see fit to impose. Only one branch of new government, the House of Representatives, was required to be elected by popular vote; and, in case popular choice of presidential electors might be established, a safeguard was secured by the indirect process. Two controlling bodies, the Senate and Supreme Court, were removed altogether from the possibility of popular election except by constitutional amendment. Finally, the conservative members of the Convention were doubly fortified in the fact that nearly all of the state constitutions then in force provided real or personal property qualifications for voters anyway, and radical democratic changes did not seem perilously near.

The Powers Conferred upon the
Federal Government

(1) The powers for positive action conferred upon the new government were few, but they were adequate to the purposes of the framers. They included, first, the power to lay and collect taxes; but here the rural interests were conciliated by the provision that direct taxes must be apportioned among the states according to population, counting three-fifths of the slaves. This, in the opinion of contemporaries eminently qualified to speak, was designed to prevent the populations of the manufacturing states from shifting the burdens of taxation to the sparsely settled agricultural regions.

In a letter to the governor of their state, three delegates from North Carolina, Blount, Spaight, and Williamson, explained the advantage of this safeguard on taxation to the southern planters and farmers: "We had many things to hope from a National Government and the chief thing we had to fear from such a Government was the risque of unequal or heavy Taxation, but we hope you will believe as we do that the Southern states in general and North Carolina in particular are well secured on that head by the proposed system. It is provided in the 9th section of article the first that no Capitation or direct Tax shall be laid except in proportion to the number of inhabitants, in which number five blacks are only counted as three. If a land tax is laid, we are to pay the same rate; for example, fifty citizens of North Carolina can be taxed no more for all their Lands than fifty Citizens in one of the Eastern States. This must be greatly in our favour, for as most of their farms are small and many of them live in Towns we certainly have, one with another, land of twice the value that they possess. When it is also considered that five Negroes are only to be charged the same Poll Tax as three whites, the advantage must be considerably increased under the proposed Form of Government. The Southern states have also a better security for the return of slaves who might endeavour to escape than they had under the original Confederation."

The taxing power was the basis of all other positive powers, and it afforded the revenues that were to discharge the public debt in full. Provision was made for this discharge in Article VI to the effect that "All debts contracted and engagements entered into before the adoption of this Constitution shall be valid against the United States under this Constitution as under the Confederation."

But the cautious student of public economy, remembering the difficulties which Congress encountered under the Articles of Confederation in its attempts to raise the money to meet the interest on the debt, may ask how the framers of the Constitution could expect to overcome the hostile economic forces which had hitherto blocked the payment of the requisitions. The answer is short. Under the Articles, Congress had no power to lay and collect taxes immediately; it could only make requisitions on the state legislatures. Inasmuch as most of the states relied largely on direct taxes for their revenues, the demands of Congress were keenly felt and stoutly resisted. Under the new system, however, Congress is authorized to lay taxes on its own account, but it is evident that the framers contemplated placing practically all of the national burden on the consumer. The provision requiring the apportionment of direct taxes on a basis of population obviously implied that such taxes were to be viewed as a last resort when indirect taxes failed to provide the required revenue.

With his usual acumen, Hamilton conciliates the freeholders and property owners in general by pointing out that they will not be called upon to support the national government by payments proportioned to their wealth. Experience has demonstrated that it is impracticable to raise any considerable sums by direct taxation. Even where the government is strong, as in Great Britain, resort must be had chiefly to indirect taxation. The pockets of the farmers "will reluctantly yield but scanty supplies, in the unwelcome shape of impositions on their houses and lands; and personal property is too precarious and invisible a fund to be laid hold of in any other way than by the imperceptible agency of taxes on consumption." Real and personal property are thus assured a generous immunity from such burdens as Congress had attempted to impose under the Articles; taxes under the new system will, therefore, be less troublesome than under the old.

(2) Congress was given, in the second place, plenary power to raise and support military and naval forces, for the defence of the country against foreign and domestic foes. These forces were to be at the disposal of the President in the execution of national laws; and to guard the states against renewed attempts of "desperate debtors" like Shays, the United States guaranteed to every commonwealth a republican form of government and promised to aid in quelling internal disorder on call of the proper authorities.

The army and navy are considered by the authors of *The Federalist* as genuine economic instrumentalities. As will be pointed out below, they regarded trade and commerce as the fundamental cause of wars between nations; and the source of domestic insurrection they traced to class conflicts within society. "Nations in general," says Jay, "will make war whenever they have a prospect of getting anything by it"; and it is obvious that the United States dissevered and discordant will be the easy prey to the commercial ambitions of their neighbors and rivals.

The material gains to be made by other nations at the expense of the United States are so apparent that the former cannot restrain themselves from aggression. France and Great Britain feel the pressure of our rivalry in the fisheries; they and other European nations are our competitors in navigation and the carrying trade; our independent voyages to China interfere with the monopolies enjoyed by other countries there; Spain would like to shut the Mississippi against us on one side and Great Britain fain would close the St. Lawrence on the other. The cheapness and excellence of our productions will excite their jealousy, and the enterprise and address of our merchants will not be consistent with wishes or policy of the sovereigns of Europe. But, adds the commentator, by way of clinching the argument, "if they see that our national government is efficient and well administered, our trade prudently regulated, our militia properly organized and disciplined, our resources and finances discreetly managed, our credit re-established, our people free, contented, and united, they will be much more disposed to cultivate our friendship than provoke our resentment."

All the powers of Europe could not prevail against us. "Under a vigorous national government the natural strength and resources of the country, directed to a common interest, would baffle all the combinations of European jealousy to restrain our growth. . . . An active commerce, an extensive navigation, and a flourishing marine would then be the offspring of moral and physical necessity. We might defy the little arts of the little politicians to control or vary the irresistible and unchangeable course of nature." In the present state of disunion the profits of trade are snatched from us; our commerce languishes; and poverty threatens to overspread a country which might outrival the world in riches.

The army and navy are to be not only instruments of defence in protecting the United States against the commercial and territorial ambitions of other countries; but they may be used also in forcing open foreign markets. What discriminatory tariffs and navigation laws may not accomplish the sword may achieve. The authors of *The Federalist* do not contemplate that policy of mild and innocuous isolation which was later made famous by Washington's farewell address. On the contrary—they do not expect the United States to change human nature and make our commercial classes less ambitious than those of other countries to extend their spheres of trade. A strong navy will command the respect of European states. "There can be no doubt that the continuance of the Union under an efficient government would put it within our power, at a period not very distant, to create a navy which, if it could not vie with those of the great maritime powers, would at least be of respectable weight if thrown into the scale of either of two contending parties. . . . A few ships of the line sent opportunely to the reinforcement of either side, would often be sufficient to decide the fate of a campaign, on the event of which interests of the greatest magnitude were suspended. Our position is, in this respect, a most commanding one. And if to this consideration we add that of the usefulness of supplies from this country, in the prosecution of military operations in the West Indies, it will be readily perceived that a situation so favorable would enable us to bargain with great advantage for commercial privileges. A price would be set not only upon our friendship, but upon our neutrality. By a steady adherence to the Union, we may hope, ere long, to become the arbiter of Europe in America, and to be able to incline the balance of European competitions in this part of the world as our interest may dictate."

As to dangers from class wars within particular states, the authors of *The Federalist* did not deem it necessary to make extended remarks: the recent events in New England were only too vividly impressed upon the public mind. "The tempestuous situation from which Massachusetts has scarcely emerged," says Hamilton, "evinces that dangers of this kind are not merely speculative. Who can determine what might have been the issue of her late convulsions, if the malcontents had been headed by a Caesar or by a Cromwell." The strong arm of the Union must be available in such crises.

In considering the importance of defense against domestic insurrection, the authors of *The Federalist* do not overlook an appeal to the slave-holders' instinctive fear of a servile revolt. Naturally, it is Madison whose interest catches this point and drives it home, by appearing to discount it. In dealing with the dangers of insurrection, he says: "I take no notice of an unhappy species of population abounding in some of the states who, during the calm of regular government are sunk below the level of men; but who, in the tempestuous scenes of civil violence, may emerge into human character and give a superiority of strength to any party with which they may associate themselves."

(3) In addition to the power to lay and collect taxes and raise and maintain armed forces on land and sea, the Constitution vests in Congress plenary control over foreign and interstate commerce, and thus authorizes it to institute protective and discriminatory laws in favor of American interests, and to create a wide sweep for free trade throughout the whole American empire. A single clause thus reflects the strong impulse of economic forces in the towns and young manufacturing centres. In a few simple words the mercantile and manufacturing interests wrote their *Zweck im Recht*; and they paid for their victory by large concessions to the slave-owning planters of the south.

While dealing with commerce in *The Federalist* Hamilton does not neglect the subject of interstate traffic and intercourse. He shows how free trade over a wide range will be to reciprocal advantage, will give great diversity to commercial enterprise, and will render stagnation less liable by offering more distant markets when local demands fall off. "The speculative trader," he concludes, "will at once perceive the force of these observations and will acknowledge that the aggregate balance of the commerce of the United States would bid fair to be much more favorable than that of the thirteen states without union or with partial unions."

(4) Another great economic antagonism found its expression in the clause conferring upon Congress the power to dispose of the territories and make rules and regulations for their government and admission to the Union. In this contest, the interests of the states which held territories came prominently to the front; and the ambiguity of the language used in the Constitution on this point may be attributed to the inability of the contestants to reach precise conclusions. The leaders were willing to risk the proper management of the land problem after the new government was safely launched; and they were correct in their estimate of their future political prowess.

These are the great powers conferred on the new government: taxation, war, commercial control, and disposition of western lands. Through them public creditors may be paid in full, domestic peace maintained, advantages obtained in dealing with foreign nations, manufactures protected, and the development of the territories go forward with full swing. The remaining powers are minor and need not be examined here. What implied powers lay in the minds of the framers likewise need not be inquired into; they have long been the subject of juridical speculation.

None of the powers conferred by the Constitution on Congress permits a direct attack on property. The federal government is given no general authority to define property. It may tax, but indirect taxes must be uniform, and these are to fall upon consumers. Direct taxes may be laid, but resort to this form of taxation is rendered practically impossible, save on extraordinary occasions, by the provision that they must be apportioned according to population—so that numbers cannot transfer the burden to accumulated wealth. The slave trade may be destroyed, it is true, after the lapse of a few years; but slavery as a domestic institution is better safeguarded than before.

Even the destruction of the slave trade had an economic basis, although much was said at the time about the ethics of the clause. In the North where slavery, though widespread, was of little economic consequence, sympathy with the unfortunate negroes could readily prevail. Maryland and Virginia, already overstocked with slaves beyond the limits of land and capital, had prohibited the foreign trade in negroes, because the slave-holders, who predominated in the legislatures, were not willing to see the value of their chattels reduced to a vanishing point by excessive importations. South Carolina and Georgia, where the death rate in the rice swamps and the opening of adjoining territories made a strong demand for the increase of slave property, on the other hand, demanded an open door for slave-dealers.

South Carolina was particularly determined, and gave northern representatives to understand that if they wished to secure their commercial privileges, they must make concessions to the slave trade. And they were met half way. Ellsworth said: "As slaves multiply so fast in Virginia and Maryland that it is cheaper to raise than import them, whilst in the sickly rice swamps foreign supplies are necessary, if we go no farther than is urged, we shall be unjust towards South Carolina and Georgia. Let us not intermeddle. As population increases; poor laborers will be so plenty as to render slaves useless."

General Pinckney taunted the Virginia representatives in the Convention, some of whom were against slavery as well as importation, with disingenuous interestedness. "South Carolina and Georgia cannot do without slaves. As to Virginia she will gain by stopping the importations. Her slaves will rise in value and she has more than she wants. It would be unequal to require South Carolina and Georgia to confederate on such unequal terms."

Restrictions Laid upon State Legislatures

Equally important to personalty as the positive powers conferred upon Congress to tax, support armies, and regulate commerce were the restrictions imposed on the states. Indeed, we have the high authority of Madison for the statement that of the forces which created the Constitution, those property interests seeking protection against omnipotent legislatures were the most active.

In a letter to Jefferson, written in October, 1787, Madison elaborates the principle of federal judicial control over state legislation, and explains the importance of this new institution in connection with the restrictions laid down in the Constitution on laws affecting private rights. "The mutability of the laws of the States," he says, "is found to be a serious evil. The injustice of them has been so frequent and so flagrant as to alarm the most steadfast friends of Republicanism. I am persuaded I do not err in saying that the evils issuing from these sources contributed more to that uneasiness which produced the Convention, and prepared the public mind for a general reform, than those which accrued to our national character and interest from the inadequacy of the Confederation to its immediate objects. A reform, therefore, which does not make provision for private rights must be materially defective."

Two small clauses embody the chief demands of personalty against agrarianism: the emission of paper money is prohibited and the states are forbidden to impair the obligation of contract. The first of these means a return to a specie basis—when coupled with the requirement that the gold and silver coin of the United States shall be the legal tender. The Shays and their paper money legions, who assaulted the vested rights of personalty by the process of legislative depreciation, are now subdued forever, and money lenders and security holders may be sure of their operations. Contracts are to be safe, and whoever engages in a financial operation, public or private, may know that state legislatures cannot destroy overnight the rules by which the game is played.

The Founding Fathers: An Age of Realism

Richard Hofstadter

Cribbing and confining the popular spirit that had been at large since 1776 were essential to the purposes of the new Constitution. Edmund Randolph, saying to the Convention that the evils from which the country suffered originated in "the turbulence and follies of democracy," and that the great danger lay in "the democratic parts of our constitutions"; Elbridge Gerry, speaking of democracy as "the worst of all political evils"; Roger Sherman, hoping that "the people . . . have as little to do as may be about the government"; William Livingston, saying that "the people have ever been and ever will be unfit to retain the exercise of power in their own hands"; George Washington, the presiding officer, urging the delegates not to produce a document of which they themselves could not approve simply in order to "please the people"; Hamilton, charging that the "turbulent and changing" masses "seldom judge or determine right" and advising a permanent governmental body to "check the imprudence of democracy"; the wealthy young planter Charles Pinckney, proposing that no one be president who was not worth at least one hundred thousand dollars—all these were quite representative of the spirit in which the problems of government were treated.

Democratic ideas are most likely to take root among discontented and oppressed classes, rising middle classes, or perhaps some sections of an old, alienated, and partially disinherited aristocracy, but they do not appeal to a privileged class that is still amplifying its privileges. With a half-dozen exceptions at the most, the men of the Philadelphia Convention were sons of men who had considerable position and wealth, and as a group they had advanced well beyond their fathers. Only one of them, William Few of Georgia, could be said in any sense to represent the yeoman farmer class which constituted the overwhelming majority of the free population. In the late eighteenth century "the better kind of people" found themselves set off from the mass by a hundred visible, tangible, and audible distinctions of dress, speech, manners, and education. There was a continuous lineage of upper-class contempt, from pre-Revolutionary Tories like Peggy Hutchinson, the Governor's daughter, who wrote one day: "The dirty mob was all about me as I drove into town," to a Federalist like Hamilton, who candidly disdained the people. Mass unrest was often received in the spirit of young Gouverneur Morris: "The mob begin to think and reason. Poor reptiles! . . . They bask in the sun, and ere noon they will bite, depend upon it. The gentry begin to fear this." Nowhere in America or Europe—not even among the great liberated thinkers of the Enlightenment—did democratic ideas appear respectable to the cultivated classes. Whether the Fathers looked to the cynically illuminated intellectuals of contemporary Europe or to their own Christian heritage of the idea of original sin, they found quick confirmation of the notion that man is an unregenerate rebel who has to be controlled.

And yet there was another side to the picture. The Fathers were intellectual heirs of seventeenth-century English republicanism with its opposition to arbitrary rule and faith in popular sovereignty. If they feared the advance of democracy, they also had misgivings about turning to the extreme right. Having recently experienced a bitter revolutionary struggle with an external power beyond their control, they were in no mood to follow Hobbes to his conclusion that any kind of government must be accepted in order to avert the anarchy and terror of a state of nature. They were uneasily aware that both military dictatorship and a return to monarchy were being seriously discussed in some quarters—the former chiefly among unpaid and discontented army officers, the latter in rich and fashionable Northern circles. John Jay, familiar with sentiment among New York's mercantile aristocracy, wrote to Washington, June 27, 1786, that he feared that "the better kind of people (by which I mean the people who are orderly and industrious, who are content with their situations, and not uneasy in their circumstances) will be led, by the insecurity of property, the loss of confidence in their rulers, and the want of public faith and rectitude, to consider the charms of liberty as imaginary and delusive." Such men, he thought, might be prepared for "almost any change that may promise them quiet and security." Washington, who had already repudiated a suggestion that he become a military dictator, agreed, remarking that "we are apt to run from one extreme to the other."

Unwilling to turn their backs upon republicanism, the Fathers also wished to avoid violating the prejudices of the people. "Notwithstanding the oppression and injustice experienced among us from democracy," said George Mason, "the genius of the people is in favor of it, and the genius of the people must be consulted." Mason admitted "that we had been too democratic," but feared that "we should incautiously run into the opposite extreme." James Madison, who has quite rightfully been called the philosopher of the Constitution, told the delegates: "It seems indispensable that the mass of citizens should not be without a voice in making the laws which they are to obey, and in choosing the magistrates who are to administer them." James Wilson, the outstanding jurist of the age, later appointed to the Supreme Court by Washington, said again and again that the ultimate power of government must of necessity reside in the people. This the Fathers commonly accepted, for if government did not proceed from the people, from what other source could it legitimately come? To adopt any other premise not only would be inconsistent with everything they had said against British rule in the past but would open the gates to an extreme concentration of power in the future. Hamilton saw the sharp distinction in the Convention when he said that "the members most tenacious of republicanism were as loud as any in declaiming the vices of democracy." There was no better expression of the dilemma of a man who has no faith in the people but insists that government be based upon them than that of Jeremy Belknap, a New England clergyman, who wrote to a friend: "Let it stand as a principle that government originates from the people; but let the people be taught . . . that they are not able to govern themselves."

It is ironical that the Constitution, which Americans venerate so deeply, is based upon a political theory that at one crucial point stands in direct antithesis to the main stream of American democratic faith. Modern American folklore assumes that democracy and liberty are all but identical, and when democratic writers take the trouble to make the distinction, they usually assume that democracy is necessary to liberty. But the Founding Fathers thought that the liberty with which they were most concerned was menaced by democracy. In their minds liberty was linked not to democracy but to property.

What did the Fathers mean by liberty? What did Jay mean when he spoke of "the charms of liberty"? Or Madison when he declared that to destroy liberty in order to destroy factions would be a remedy worse than the disease? Certainly the men who met at Philadelphia were not interested in extending liberty to those classes in America, the Negro slaves and the indentured servants, who were most in need of it, for slavery was recognized in the organic structure of the Constitution and indentured servitude was no concern of the Convention. Nor was the regard of the delegates for civil liberties any too tender. It was the opponents of the Constitution who were most active in demanding such vital liberties as freedom of religion, freedom of speech and press, jury trial, due process, and protection from "unreasonable searches and seizures." These guarantees had to be incorporated in the first ten amendments because the Convention neglected to put them in the original document. Turning to economic issues, it was not freedom of trade in the modern sense that the Fathers were striving for. Although they did not believe in impeding trade unnecessarily, they felt that failure to regulate it was one of the central weaknesses of the Articles of Confederation, and they stood closer to the mercantilists than to Adam Smith. Again, liberty to them did not mean free access to the nation's unappropriated wealth. At least fourteen of them were land speculators. They did not believe in the right of the squatter to occupy unused land, but rather in the right of the absentee owner or speculator to pre-empt it.

The liberties that the constitutionalists hoped to gain were chiefly negative. They wanted freedom from fiscal uncertainty and irregularities in the currency, from trade wars among the states, from economic discrimination by more powerful foreign governments, from attacks on the creditor class or on property, from popular insurrection. They aimed to create a government that would act as an honest broker among a variety of propertied interests, giving them all protection from their common enemies and preventing any one of them from becoming too powerful. The Convention was a fraternity of types of absentee ownership. All property should be permitted to have its proportionate voice in government. Individual property interests might have to be sacrificed at times, but only for the community of propertied interests. Freedom for property would result in liberty for men—perhaps not for all men, but at least for all worthy men. Because men have different faculties and abilities, the Fathers believed, they acquire different amounts of property. To protect property is only to protect men in the exercise of their natural faculties. Among the many liberties, therefore, freedom to hold and dispose of property is paramount. Democracy, unchecked rule by the masses, is sure to bring arbitrary redistribution of property, destroying the very essence of liberty.

The Fathers' conception of democracy, shaped by their practical experience with the aggressive dirt farmers in the American states and the urban mobs of the Revolutionary period, was supplemented by their reading in history and political science. Fear of what Madison called "the superior force of an interested and overbearing majority" was the dominant emotion aroused by their study of historical examples. The chief examples of republics were among the city-states of antiquity, medieval Europe, and early modern times. Now, the history of these republics—a history, as Hamilton said, "of perpetual vibration between the extremes of tyranny and anarchy"—was alarming. Further, most of the men who had overthrown the liberties of republics had "begun their career by paying an obsequious court to the people; commencing demagogues and ending tyrants."

All the constitutional devices that the Fathers praised in their writings were attempts to guarantee the future of the United States against the "turbulent" political cycles of previous republics. By "democracy," they meant a system of government which directly expressed the will of the majority of the people, usually through such an assemblage of the people as was possible in the small area of the city-state.

A cardinal tenet in the faith of the men who made the Constitution was the belief that democracy can never be more than a transitional stage in government, that it always evolves into either a tyranny (the rule of the rich demagogue who has patronized the mob) or an aristocracy (the original leaders of the democratic elements). "Remember," wrote the dogmatic John Adams in one of his letters to John Taylor of Caroline, "democracy never lasts long. It soon wastes, exhausts, and murders itself. There never was a democracy yet that did not commit suicide." Again:

> If you give more than a share in the sovereignty to the democrats, that is, if you give them the command or preponderance in the ... legislature, they will vote all property out of the hands of you aristocrats, and if they let you escape with your lives, it will be more humanity, consideration, and generosity than any triumphant democracy ever displayed since the creation. And what will follow? The aristocracy among the democrats will take your places, and treat their fellows as severely and sternly as you have treated them.

Government, thought the Fathers, is based on property. Men who have no property lack the necessary stake in an orderly society to make stable or reliable citizens. Dread of the propertyless masses of the towns was all but universal. George Washington, Gouverneur Morris, John Kickinson, and James Madison spoke of their anxieties about the urban working class that might arise some time in the future—"men without property and principle," as Dickinson described them—and even the democratic Jefferson shared this prejudice. Madison, stating the problem, came close to anticipating the modern threats to conservative republicanism from both communism and fascism:

In future times, a great majority of the people will not only be without landed but any other sort of property. These will either combine, under the influence of their common situation—in which case the rights of property and the public liberty will not be secure in their hands—or, what is more probable, they will become the tools of opulence and ambition, in which case there will be equal danger on another side.

What encouraged the Fathers about their own era, however, was the broad dispersion of landed property. The small land-owning farmers had been troublesome in recent years, but there was a general conviction that under a properly made Constitution a *modus vivendi* could be worked out with them. The possession of moderate plots of property presumably gave them a sufficient stake in society to be safe and responsible citizens under the restraints of balanced government. Influence in government would be proportionate to property: merchants and great landholders would be dominant, but small property-owners would have an independent and far from negligible voice. It was "politic as well as just," said Madison, "that the interests and rights of every class should be duly represented and understood in the public councils," and John Adams declared that there could be "no free government without a democratical branch in the constitution."

The farming element already satisfied the property requirements for suffrage in most of the states, and the Fathers generally had no quarrel with their enfranchisement. But when they spoke of the necessity of founding government upon the consent of "the people," it was only these small property-holders that they had in mind. For example, the famous Virginia Bill of Rights, written by George Mason, explicitly defined those eligible for suffrage as all men "having sufficient evidence of permanent common interest with and attachment to the community"—which meant, in brief, sufficient property.

However, the original intention of the Fathers to admit the yeoman into an important but sharply limited partnership in affairs of state could not be perfectly realized. At the time the Constitution was made, Southern planters and Northern merchants were setting their differences aside in order to meet common dangers—from radicals within and more powerful nations without. After the Constitution was adopted, conflict between the ruling classes broke out anew, especially after powerful planters were offended by the favoritism of Hamilton's policies to Northern commercial interests. The planters turned to the farmers to form an agrarian alliance, and for more than half a century this powerful coalition embraced the bulk of the articulate interests of the country. As time went on, therefore, the main stream of American political conviction deviated more and more from the antidemocratic position of the Constitution-makers. Yet, curiously, their general satisfaction with the Constitution together with their growing nationalism made Americans deeply reverent of the founding generation, with the result that as it grew stronger, this deviation was increasingly overlooked.

Bibliography

Seymour Martin Lipset, *The First New Nation* (New York: Anchor Doubleday, 1963.) Part 1 deals with the period during which the constitutional convention was held. Lipset's approach is to compare America's first elites with elites in modern emerging nations.

Clinton Rossiter, *1787, The Grand Convention* (New York, Mentor, 1966). Rossiter carefully documents the elitist composition of the constitutional convention.

Forrest McDonald, *We the People* (Chicago: Chicago University Press, 1963). An attack on Charles Beard's economic interpetation of the constitution and a reaffirmation of the democratic character of that document.

**The Few Who
Have Power:
Elites in America**

Power in America is organized into large private and public institutions: corporations, banks and financial institutions, universities, law firms, churches, professional associations, and military and governmental bureaucracies. America's powerful men are those who occupy the top positions in those institutions, because they control the nation's resources.

An elitist interpretation of power in contemporary America emphasizes the following ideas:

(1) High positions in industry, finance, government, education, and the military involve control over the nation's resources and have, therefore, great potential for power.

(2) Power is exercised when the institutional structure of society limits the scope of public decision-making so as to prevent the consideration of issues which are seriously detrimental to the values and interests of the elite.

(3) Elites are recruited disproportionately from the upper socio-economic classes in society.

(4) There is considerable overlap in high elite positions. Top governmental elites are generally recruited from key posts in private industry and finance, and these same men have also often held influential positions in education, arts and sciences, and social, civic, and charitable associations.

(5) Economic power is increasingly concentrated in the hands of those few men who occupy key posts in giant corporations.

(6) The economic system is inextricably intertwined with the political system. No clear division exists between governmental, business, and military enterprise.

In his influential book *The Power Elite*, sociologist C. Wright Mills argues persuasively that power in America is concentrated at the top of the nation's giant corporate and governmental organizations, and that corporate, governmental, and military bureaucracies closely interlock to form a single structure of power. It is these institutions, and the men who guide them, that shape the lives of everyone.

Fortune Magazine tries to keep track of America's men of wealth, the "centimillionaires." They find that it is still possible to build a great fortune very rapidly in this land of opportunity. However, most of the great private wealth in America has been held by a very few families for generations. "The notion that du Ponts, Fords, Mellons, and Rockefellers are among America's wealthiest citizens happens to be true."

Political scientist Donald Matthews, in the now classic study, *The Social Background of Political Decision-Makers*, provides convincing evidence that America's governmental leaders are drawn from the upper socio-economic strata of society. "The log cabin to White House myth is rather far from the truth. . . . For the most part political decision-makers are far from common men, in either their origins, or their achievements." Professor Matthews documents these conclusions with data on the background of presidents, vice presidents, cabinet officials, high-level civil servants, U.S. Senators and Congressmen, and state governors and legislators. However, at the end of his study, he has added a little essay discounting the importance of his own findings. True to the pluralist tradition, Professor Matthews argues that the class character of America's decision-makers is largely irrelevant and simply reflects the natural process of political recruitment in America. He also argues that the unrepresentative nature of America's political decision-makers does not free them from their accountability to the electorate.

Economist, diplomat, and presidential advisor John K. Galbraith, whose own elite credentials are impeccable, describes the interrelatedness of the corporate and governmental "technostructure" in *The New Industrial State*. Government and business, he observes, are not really competitive. The modern corporation and the state are inextricably associated with each other. The line between public and private authority in America is "indistinct and in large measure imaginary." But he acknowledges that "this runs strongly counter to the accepted doctrine" of pluralism, but proceeds to accurately analyze the interdependent and non-competitive corporate and state relationships in America.

In a thoughtful book on the American military, entitled *The Professional Soldier*, sociologist Morris Janowitz carefully reviews the image and the reality of the modern military establishment. Janowitz observes that the traditional, stern, ethnocentric, narrow, authoritarian, military leader has been replaced in modern times by a highly skilled, technically competent, management-oriented, politically aware, public-relations-conscious, organizational leader. "There has been a change in the basis of authority and discipline in the military establishment, a shift from authoritarian domination to greater reliance on manipulation, persuasion, and group consensus." There has been a narrowing of differences between military and corporate and governmental leadership. The traditional "military mind," so frequently ridiculed by liberal commentators, is no longer an accurate portrait of the modern professional military leader. But the passing of the traditional military figure may mean *more* rather than *less* military influence in national affairs, because the new professional soldier is much more conscious of his broad relationship with government and society. "As a result of the complex machinery of warfare which has weakened the line between military and non-military organization, the military establishment has come to display more and more the characteristics typical of any large scale organization."

The Higher Circles

C. Wright Mills

Within American society, major national power now resides in the economic, the political, and the military domains. Other institutions seem off to the side of modern history, and, on occasion, duly subordinated to these. No family is as directly powerful in national affairs as any major corporation; no church is as directly powerful in the external biographies of young men in America today as the military establishment; no college is as powerful in the shaping of momentous events as the National Security Council. Religious, educational and family institutions are not autonomous centers of national power; on the contrary, these decentralized areas are increasingly shaped by the big three, in which developments of decisive and immediate consequence now occur.

Families and churches and schools adapt to modern life; governments and armies and corporations shape it; and, as they do so, they turn these lesser institutions into means for their ends. Religious institutions provide chaplains to the armed forces where they are used as a means of increasing the effectiveness of its morale to kill. Schools select and train men for their jobs in corporations and their specialized tasks in the armed forces. The extended family has, of course, long been broken up by the industrial revolution, and now the son and the father are removed from the family, by compulsion if need be, whenever the army of the state sends out the call. And the symbols of all these lesser institutions are used to legitimate the power and the decisions of the big three.

The life-fate of the modern individual depends not only upon the family into which he was born or which he enters by marriage, but increasingly upon the corporation in which he spends the most alert hours of his best years; not only upon the school where he is educated as a child and adolescent but also upon the state which touches him throughout his life; not only upon the church in which on occasion he hears the word of God, but also upon the army in which he is disciplined.

If the centralized state could not rely upon the inculcation of nationalist loyalties in public and private schools, its leaders would promptly seek to modify the decentralized educational system. If the bankruptcy rate among the top five hundred corporations were as high as the general divorce rate among the thirty-seven million married couples, there would be economic catastrophe on an international scale. If members of armies gave to them no more of their lives than do believers to the churches to which they belong, there would be a military crisis.

Within each of the big three, the typical institutional unit has become enlarged, has become administrative, and, in the power of its decisions, has become centralized. Behind these developments there is a fabulous technology, for as institutions, they have incorporated this technology and guide it, even as it shapes and paces their developments.

The economy—once a great scatter of small productive units in autonomous balance—has become dominated by two or three hundred giant corporations, administratively and politically interrelated, which together hold the keys to economic decisions.

The political order, once a decentralized set of several dozen states with a weak spinal cord, has become a centralized, executive establishment which has taken up into itself many powers previously scattered, and now enters into each and every cranny of the social structure.

The military order, once a slim establishment in a context of distrust fed by state militia, has become the largest and most expensive feature of government, and, although well versed in smiling public relations, now has all the grim and clumsy efficiency of a sprawling bureaucratic domain.

In each of these institutional areas, the means of power at the disposal of decision makers have increased enormously; their central executive powers have been enhanced; within each of them modern administrative routines have been elaborated and tightened up.

As each of these domains becomes enlarged and centralized, the consequences of its activities become greater, and its traffic with the others increases. The decisions of a handful of corporations bear upon military and political as well as upon economic developments around the world. The decisions of the military establishment rest upon and grievously affect political life as well as the very level of economic activity. The decisions made within the political domain determine economic activities and military programs. There is no longer, on the one hand, an economy, and, on the other hand, a political order containing a military establishment unimportant to politics and to money-making. There is a political economy linked, in a thousand ways, with military institutions and decisions. On each side of the world-split running through central Europe and around the Asiatic rimlands, there is an ever-increasing interlocking of economic, military, and political structures. If there is government intervention in the corporate economy, so is there corporate intervention in the governmental process. In the structural sense, this triangle of power is the source of the interlocking directorate that is most important for the historical structure of the present.

The fact of the interlocking is clearly revealed at each of the points of crisis of modern capitalist society—slump, war, and boom. In each, men of decision are led to an awareness of the interdependence of the major institutional orders. In the nineteenth century, when the scale of all institutions was smaller, their liberal integration was achieved in the automatic economy, by an autonomous play of market forces, and in the automatic political domain, by the bargain and the vote. It was then assumed that out of the imbalance and friction that followed the limited decisions then possible a new equilibrium would in due course emerge. That can no longer be assumed, and it is not assumed by the men at the top of each of the three dominant hierarchies.

For given the scope of their consequences, decisions—and indecisions—in any one of these ramify into the others, and hence top decisions tend either to become co-ordinated or to lead to a commanding indecision. It has not always been like this. When numerous small entrepreneurs made up the economy, for example, many of them could fail and the consequences still remain local;

political and military authorities did not intervene. But now, given political expectations and military commitments, can they afford to allow key units of the private corporate economy to break down in slump? Increasingly, they do intervene in economic affairs, and as they do so, the controlling decisions in each order are inspected by agents of the other two, and economic, military, and political structures are interlocked.

At the pinnacle of each of the three enlarged and centralized domains, there have arisen those higher circles which make up the economic, the political, and the military elites. At the top of the economy, among the corporate rich, there are the chief executives; at the top of the political order, the members of the political directorate; at the top of the military establishment, the elite of soldier-statesmen clustered in and around the Joint Chiefs of Staff and the upper echelon. As each of these domains has coincided with the others, as decisions tend to become total in their consequences, the leading men in each of the three domains of power—the warlords, the corporation chieftains, the political directorate—tend to come together, to form the power elite of America.

The higher circles in and around these command posts are often thought of in terms of what their members possess: they have a greater share than other people of the things and experiences that are most highly valued. From this point of view, the elite are simply those who have the most of what there is to have, which is generally held to include money, power, and prestige—as well as all the ways of life to which these lead. But the elite are not simply those who have the most, for they could not 'have the most' were it not for their positions in the great institutions. For such institutions are the necessary bases of power, of wealth, and of prestige, and at the same time, the chief means of exercising power, of acquiring and retaining wealth, and of cashing in the higher claims for prestige.

By the powerful we mean, of course, those who are able to realize their will, even if others resist it. No one, accordingly, can be truly powerful unless he has access to the command of major institutions, for it is over these institutional means of power that the truly powerful are, in the first instance, powerful. Higher politicians and key officials of government command such institutional power; so do admirals and generals, and so do the major owners and executives of the larger corporations. Not all power, it is true, is anchored in and exercised by means of such institutions, but only within and through them can power be more or less continuous and important.

Wealth also is acquired and held in and through institutions. The pyramid of wealth cannot be understood merely in terms of the very rich; for the great inheriting families, as we shall see, are now supplemented by the corporate institutions of modern society: every one of the very rich families has been and is closely connected—always legally and frequently managerially as well—with one of the multi-million dollar corporations.

The modern corporation is the prime source of wealth, but, in latter-day capitalism, the political apparatus also opens and closes many avenues to wealth. The amount as well as the source of income, the power over consumer's goods as well as over productive capital, are determined by position within the political economy. If our interest in the very rich goes beyond their lavish or their miserly consumption, we must examine their relations to modern forms of corporate property as well as to the state; for such relations now determine the chances of men to secure big property and to receive high income.

Great prestige increasingly follows the major institutional units of the social structure. It is obvious that prestige depends, often quite decisively, upon access to the publicity machines that are now a central and normal feature of all the big institutions of modern America. Moreover, one feature of these hierarchies of corporation, state, and military establishment is that their top positions are increasingly interchangeable. One result of this is the accumulative nature of prestige. Claims for prestige, for example, may be initially based on military roles, then expressed in and augmented by an educational institution run by corporate executives, and cashed in, finally, in the political order, where, for General Eisenhower and those he represents, power and prestige finally meet at the very peak. Like wealth and power, prestige tends to be cumulative: the more of it you have, the more you can get. These values also tend to be translatable into one another: the wealthy find it easier than the poor to gain power; those with status find it easier than those without it to control opportunities for wealth.

If we took the one hundred most powerful men in America, the one hundred wealthiest, and the one hundred most celebrated away from the institutional positions they now occupy, away from their resources of men and women and money, away from the media of mass communication that are now focused upon them—then they would be powerless and poor and uncelebrated. For power is not of a man. Wealth does not center in the person of the wealthy. Celebrity is not inherent in any personality. To be celebrated, to be wealthy, to have power requires access to major institutions, for the institutional positions men occupy determine in large part their chances to have and to hold these valued experiences.

America's Centimillionaires

Arthur M. Louis

The U.S. has become so affluent that there no longer is any great prestige in being a mere millionaire. The very word "millionaire" is seldom used nowadays: indeed, it has an almost quaint sound. It belongs to the era some decades back when a net worth of $1 million was considered a "fortune": a millionaire was a member of a small class, and therefore a natural object of curiosity. To have a net worth of $1 million today is to be, much of the time, indistinguishable from members of the omnipresent middle class.

How many Americans are now wealthy enough to be thought of roughly as we once thought of millionaires? How many command the means to live—by the demanding standards of the late 1960's—in spectacular luxury? How many have the power, if not necessarily the inclination, to intervene decisively in sizable business deals? When *Fortune* looked at the Super Rich in 1957, it drew the line at $50 million. (See "The Fifty-Million-Dollar Man," November, 1957.) At that time, it appeared, 155 individuals were over the line. Today, partly because of inflation but mainly because much higher standards seem appropriate, the cut-off figure must be doubled. The question, then, is how many Americans are worth at least $100 million.

In the 1957 article it was estimated that forty-five of the 155 were worth $100 million or more. Today, after a four-month study that entailed analysis of public records (e.g., proxy statements) and hundreds of interviews, we believe we can identify 153 individuals whose net worth, including wealth held by their spouses, minor children, trusts, and foundations, makes them centimillionaires. (Neither compilation can be considered definitive, however; some forms of wealth—and some of the Super Rich themselves—absolutely defy detection.) A sizable minority—perhaps a third—were men of modest means and obscure reputation a decade ago; i.e., they did not come close to making the 1957 list. Despite their immense wealth, some of them remain obscure even today. Indeed, it seems likely that most readers will find names in this article (and in the list beginning on page 66, which includes sixty-six individuals estimated to have at least $150 million) that are entirely new to them, and other names that they had never associated with nine-digit fortunes.

One finding, then, is that it is still possible to build a great fortune rapidly, and starting from a very low base. However, heirs and heiresses are well represented in the list on page 156; about half of the people with $150 million or more inherited the bulk of it. The notion that du Ponts, Fords, Mellons, and Rockefellers are among America's wealthiest citizens happens to be true.

Returns on Ingenuity

Of the self-made centimillionaires, one of the wealthiest of all is Dr. Edwin H. Land, fifty-eight, founder and chairman of Polaroid Corp. Dr. Land's financial position was extremely precarious not so long ago, and it often appeared that a little bad luck would be enough to overwhelm Polaroid. During the 1940's, as he worked endless hours to develop the sixty-second camera, his company went into a frightening decline. Toward the end of 1948, when the camera finally was placed on the market, Polaroid's annual sales had dropped to $1,500,000, less than a tenth of their level three years earlier, and the company was suffering its third large deficit in a row. The stock also was weak; Dr Land's controlling interest was worth only about $1,500,000. What has happened since is one of the great miracles of business, fully documented and widely publicized, but still awesome to contemplate. The camera became a smashing success, the company's sales increased over two-hundredfold, and the inventor's wealth increased even more. Dr. Land and his wife now hold around a half-billion dollars' worth of Polaroid stock.

While Dr. Land's achievement was exceptionally dramatic and lucrative, one can cite many other modern-day entrepreneurs who entered the marketplace with little more than their ingenuity and daring, and proceeded to reap stupendous returns; here are just a few:

David Packard, fifty-five, and *William R. Hewlett*, fifty-four, chairman and president respectively of the Hewlett-Packard Co., went into business in 1939, after earning their electrical-engineering degrees at Stanford University. Hewlett had developed a new type of audio oscillator while studying at Stanford, and the partners later sold eight to the Walt Disney studios, which used them to produce sound effects for *Fantasia*. The pair's capital investment at the start was only $538, including a drill press, which they operated in Packard's one-car garage. Hewlett-Packard today is a leading manufacturer of electronic measuring instruments (sales last year were $243 million), and its founders are ensconced high among the Super Rich; each owns a quarter-billion dollars' worth of stock. As recently as the mid-1950's, Hewlett and Packard spent much of their time tinkering in the company's laboratories; but as the business grew, they confined themselves largely to administrative chores. Hewlett still devotes a lot of attention to the development of products, while Packard, as chief executive officer, concentrates on general business matters.

W. Clement Stone, sixty-five, went into the insurance business while still in his teens, bringing to the venture scant capital but a large talent for salesmanship. It was a one-man operation until he married Jessie Tarson in 1923; after that, Mrs. Stone prepared and mailed the correspondence while Stone was out selling. Today his firm, the Combined Insurance Co. of America, has more than a thousand employees, and $142 million in assets. Its stock has soared since it was offered to the public six and a half years ago, and the holdings of Stone, his wife, and their foundation recently totaled $130 million. Stone has given his family shares worth another $127 million, and his other investments amount to perhaps $70 million more. Some of Stone's fellow Chicagoans find him refreshingly free of countinghouse mannerisms, and wonder that he could have made so much money. He explains that he was inspired early in life by a "self-help" book, which taught him "the art of self-motivation." Stone now can write that sort of book himself—and in fact he has. He is the author of one entitled *The Success System That Never Fails*, and co-author of another entitled *Success Through a Positive Mental Attitude*.

O. Wayne Rollins, fifty-five, chairman and president of Rollins, Inc., started a radio station in tiny Georgetown, Delaware, twenty years ago, after his brother John, who sold cars there, complained that he had no place to advertise. The Rollins broadcasting chain has since grown to eight radio stations and three television stations, mostly on the Atlantic seaboard, and the company has diversified into outdoor advertising, cosmetics, building maintenance, and pest control; revenues last year were $78 million. Rollins, who was born on a farm in Ringgold, Georgia, worked for ten years in the laboratory of a textile mill in nearby Chattanooga, Tennessee, after his graduation from high school. The job finally repelled him because, as he explains: "So much of your work is thrown away. I place too much value on time and money." He later spent five years supervising the production of TNT for Hercules, and he was operating the Catoosa Mineral Springs, a Georgia resort, when he decided to go into broadcasting. Rollins has avidly purchased real estate through the years, most notably—and presciently—in Florida, and now reckons his fortune at well over $100 million, some $70 million of it in his company's stock, which is listed on the American Stock Exchange.

E. Claiborne Robins, fifty-seven, took over the family drug company, A. H. Robins, in 1933, after his graduation from pharmacy school. The company had been barely kept alive by his widowed mother; sales in that depression-ridden year were only $4,800. Under his guidance, A. H. Robins began doing its own research, and diversified into pet foods and cosmetics (Chap Stick); last year the sales reached $100 million. Robins is celebrated for his paternal devotion to his employees. In 1957 he took them all—there were 132 at the time—to Havana for a five-day vacation. While he no longer can offer that particular fringe benefit, he does send each one—they now number more than 2,000—birthday and Christmas presents. When A. H. Robins went public in 1963, part of the offering was reserved for the employees; the stock has since tripled in price. Robins and his family, while they have sold a third of their original holdings, still own well over $200 million worth.

As these examples suggest, the great new fortunes are being made in much the same manner as the great old ones. It still is necessary to enter a business at or near the ground floor, to hold a major interest in the stock, and to resist selling during hard times. One significant change is that the new fortunes are being made in entirely different industries. The wealth of many of today's Super Rich *heirs* originally came from automobiles, chemicals, food processing, oil, railroading, and steel—industries that now are basic, and no longer growing rapidly. The new fortunes are coming from industries that are still growing rapidly, but seem destined to become basic—e.g., communications, drugs and cosmetics, insurance, and the various high-technology industries.

The high-technology companies are producing rich proprietors with astonishing speed. Because these companies are relatively new, only a few of their proprietors currently are centimillionaires. But it seems plain that many more eventually will be, as the goods and services they provide become essential to the economy. Investors already are paying generously for dozens of companies with intriguing prospects but brief histories, and one can point to several individuals who are worth scores of millions, but were worth very little a few years (or even months) ago. An arresting example is Dr. An Wang, forty-eight, who founded Wang Laboratories, a computer manufacturer, in 1951, three years after getting his Ph.D. degree at Harvard. Dr. Wang, a native of Shanghai offered some stock to the public last August at $12.50 a share, or twenty-five times earnings for the fiscal year ending June 30, 1967. By late October, investors had bid the price up to $81, boosting the value of the shares held by Wang, his wife, and their trust to $92 million. More recently, their holdings were worth $60 million. William C. Norris, fifty-seven, who founded Control Data Corp. only eleven years ago, saw his holdings grow to $67 million last December, when investors were appraising the company at well over a hundred times its earnings for fiscal 1967. By mid-March, however, his shares were worth only $45 million.

Because the high-technology stocks are so volatile, they provide an uncertain foundation for a great fortune. The riskiest common stocks generally are those with the highest price-earnings ratios; in the market slump early this year, for example, the so-called "glamour" issues fell much more sharply than most other stocks. Even Dr. Land, whose company's stock recently was selling at more than fifty times last year's earnings, received a severe jolt. He and his wife watched the value of their Polaroid holdings decline by $198 million between early December and mid-March, including a plunge of more than $42 million *in a single day* during February. Howard Vollum and M. J. Murdock, co-founders of Tektronix, a manufacturer of cathode-ray oscilloscopes, each held more than $115 million worth of their company's stock in October; by mid-March the same holdings were worth less than $77 million each. J. Erik Jonsson, sixty-six, former chairman of Texas Instruments and currently the mayor of Dallas, had $100 million worth of T.I. stock in October, but saw his stake shrink to less than $70 million in February, when the company disclosed that its earnings per share had fallen 33 percent last year. And Charles B. (Tex) Thornton, chairman of Litton Industries, whose company also has had earnings problems, watched his holdings drop from $147 million in October to $79 million by mid-March.

Precipitous stock-market declines are not limited to high-priced, high-technology stocks. When a company runs into sudden trouble, as Texas Instruments and Litton did, the market usually reacts ferociously; and anyone who has a large fortune bound up in that company may see it decimated as swiftly as it was built. This lesson recently was brought home to Edward J. Daly, forty-five, who eighteen years ago paid $50,000 in cash for World Airways, a charter airline. The company flourished, and Daly made a public offering in April, 1966. The value of Daly's holdings rose from $100 million at the time of the offering to $337 million last July; then the stock went into a nose dive, and in the next eight months Daly lost more than $200 million in paper profits.

The Richest of the Rich

$1 Billion to $1.5 Billion

J. Paul Getty, seventy-five; Californian living in England; Getty Oil Co.
Howard Hughes, sixty-two; Las Vegas; Hughes Aircraft, Hughes Tool, real estate

$500 Million to $1 Billion

H. L. Hunt, seventy-nine; Dallas; independent oil operator
Dr. Edwin H. Land, fifty-eight; Cambridge, Massachusetts; Polaroid
Daniel K. Ludwig, seventy; New York; shipping
Ailsa Mellon Bruce, sixty-six; New York
Paul Mellon, sixty; Upperville, Virginia
Richard King Mellon, sixty-eight; Pittsburgh

N. Bunker Hunt, forty-two; Dallas; independent oil operator; son of H. L. Hunt

John D. MacArthur, seventy-one; Chicago and Palm Beach; Bankers Life & Casualty

William L. McKnight, eighty; St. Paul, Minnesota; Minnesota Mining & Manufacturing

Charles S. Mott, ninety-two; Flint, Michigan; General Motors

R. E. (Bob) Smith, seventy-three; Houston: independent oil operator, real estate

$200 Million to $300 Million

Howard F. Ahmanson, sixty-one; Los Angeles; Home Savings & Loan Association

Charles Allen Jr., sixty-five; New York; investment banking

Mrs. W. Van Alan Clark Sr. (Edna McConnell), eighty; New York and Hobe Sound; Avon Products

John T. Dorrance Jr., forty-nine; Philadelphia; Campbell Soup

Mrs. Alfred I. du Pont, eighty-four; Jacksonville

Charles W. Engelhard Jr., fifty-one; Newark, New Jersey; mining and metal fabricating

Sherman M. Fairchild, seventy-two; New York; Fairchild Camera, I.B.M.

Leon Hess, fifty-four; New York; Hess Oil & Chemical

William R. Hewlett, fifty-four; Palo Alto; Hewlett-Packard

David Packard, fifty-five; Palo Alto; Hewlett-Packard

Amory Houghton, sixty-eight; Corning, New York; Corning Glass Works

Joseph P. Kennedy, seventy-nine; Palm Beach

Eli Lilly, eighty-three; Indianapolis; Eli Lilly & Co.

Forrest E. Mars, sixty-four; Washington; Mars candy

Samuel I. Newhouse, seventy-three; New York; newspapers

Marjorie Merriweather Post, eighty-one; Washington and Palm Beach; General Foods

Mrs. Jean Mauze (Abby Rockefeller), sixty-four; New York

David Rockefeller, fifty-two; New York

John D. Rockefeller III, sixty-two; New York

Laurance Rockefeller, fifty-seven; New York

Nelson Rockefeller, fifty-nine; New York

Winthrop Rockefeller, fifty-six; Little Rock, Arkansas

Cordelia Scaife May, thirty-nine; Pittsburgh; Mellon family

Richard Mellon Scaife, thirty-five; Pittsburgh

DeWitt Wallace, seventy-eight; Chappaqua, New York; *Reader's Digest*

Mrs. Charles Payson (Joan Whitney), sixty-five; New York

John Hay Whitney, sixty-three; New York

$150 Million to $200 Million

James S. Abercrombie, seventy-six; Houston; independent oil operator, Cameron Iron Works

William Benton, sixty-eight; New York; *Encyclopaedia Britannica*

Jacob Blaustein, seventy-five; Baltimore; Standard Oil of Indiana

Chester Carlson, sixty-two; Rochester, New York; inventor of xerography

Edward J. Daly, forty-five; Oakland; World Airways

Clarence Dillon, eighty-five; New York; investment banking

Doris Duke, fifty-five; New York

Lammot du Pont Copeland, sixty-two; Wilmington

Henry B. du Pont, sixty-nine; Wilmington

Benson Ford, forty-eight; Detroit; Ford Motor

Mrs. W. Buhl Ford II (Josephine Ford), forty-four; Detroit; Ford Motor

William C. Ford, forty-three; Detroit; Ford Motor

Helen Clay Frick, seventy-nine; Pittsburgh; daughter of Henry Clay Frick

William T. Grant, ninety-one; New York; W. T. Grant variety stores

Bob Hope, sixty-four; Hollywood

Arthur A. Houghton Jr., sixty-one; New York; Corning Glass Works

J. Seward Johnson, seventy-two; New Brunswick, New Jersey; Johnson & Johnson

Peter Kiewit, sixty-seven; Omaha; construction

Allan P. Kirby, seventy-five; Morristown, New Jersey; Woolworth heir, Alleghany Corp.

J. S. McDonnell Jr., sixty-nine; St. Louis; McDonnell Douglas, aircraft

Mrs. Lester J. Norris (Dellora F. Angell), sixty-five; St. Charles, Illinois; niece of John W. (Bet-a-Million) Gates

E. Claiborne Robins, fifty-seven; Richmond; A. H. Robins, drugs

W. Clement Stone, sixty-five; Chicago; insurance

Mrs. Arthur Hays Sulzberger (Iphigene Ochs), seventy-five; New York; *New York Times*

S. Mark Taper, sixty-six; Los Angeles; First Charter Financial Corp.

Robert W. Woodruff, seventy-eight; Atlanta; Coca-Cola

The two richest Americans are J. Paul Getty, seventy-five, and Howard Hughes, sixty-two, the only ones who probably can be called billionaires. But it is impossible to say which is richer.

The issue remains in doubt because both men have substantial assets that cannot be precisely evaluated. Perhaps half of Hughes's wealth is in two privately held companies. He owns all the stock of Hughes Tool Co., while the stock of Hughes Aircraft Co. belongs to the Howard Hughes Medical Institute, a foundation he created; neither company, of course, has a quoted market value. In addition, both Getty and Hughes own large amounts of real estate, a type of asset that also is difficult to evaluate; an estimate normally is based on the most recent sale of comparable parcels, but the actual value cannot be determined unless the real estate is placed on the market.

There is, however, a market value for the bulk of Getty's wealth—his holdings in Getty Oil Co. The stock recently was selling for $82.50 a share. But it is conceivable that the company, if liquidated, would bring as much as $150 per share. And since Getty, as either owner or trustee, controls 62 percent of the company, he is in a position to liquidate. Getty owns 4,600,917 shares of Getty Oil directly, and is an income beneficiary of the Sarah C. Getty Trust, named for his late mother, which owns 7,948,272 shares. Getty is the only trustee, but 20.7 percent of the trust is in the names of his four sons, all adults. At $82.50 a share, Getty's direct holdings were worth $379,575,652, and his interest in the trust shares was worth $519,995,825, for a total of $899,571,477. However, if the same shares were liquidated at $150 each, his total would be $1,635,584,504, minus a capital-gains tax of perhaps $400 million, which would leave $1,235,584,504.

Getty's other visible assets are slender by comparison. His art collection is probably worth between $20 million and $50 million. His museum in Malibu is worth between $5 million and $10 million. Other real estate is worth perhaps $30 million to $40 million. Getty also recently owned, directly and through the Sarah C. Getty Trust, $2,832,812 worth of stock in Spartan Aircraft.

This, then, is how the most conservative, and the most liberal, estimates of Getty's *visible* assets would look:

Assets	Conservative Evaluation	Liberal Evaluation
Getty Oil Co. stock	$899,571,477	$1,235,584,504
Art Museum and collection	25,000,000	60,000,000
Other real estate	30,000,000	40,000,000
Spartan Aircraft Co. stock	2,832,812	2,832,812
Total	$957,404,289	$1,338,417,316

Calculations of Hughes's wealth naturally require more guesswork. His companies, for example, do not report either sales or earnings. Hughes Aircraft has sales of about $620 million, mostly to the military and the National Aeronautics and Space Administration. Government contracts entail low profit margins, and the company also has been less profit-minded than other aerospace firms. It seems fair to estimate Hughes Aircraft's actual earnings at $12,500,000; but in different hands the company might be earning $25 million. At fifteen times these two earnings figures, Hughes Aircraft would therefore be worth between $187,500,000 and $375 million.

As for Hughes Tool, the available evidence suggests a minimum hypothetical market value of $200 million, and a maximum of $300 million, excluding certain substantial investments that Howard Hughes has made in the company's name. His 75 percent interest in Trans World Airlines, for example, which he sold in May, 1966, was held in the name of Hughes Tool.

Hughes has received substantial cash proceeds from the sale of publicly held stock. The T.W.A. sale yielded $546,549,771, of which perhaps $436 million was left after payment of the capital-gains tax. Hughes also got about $11 million when he sold his interest in Northeast Airlines three years ago. He has invested about $100 million in hotels, two private airports, and land in or near Las Vegas, and some, though perhaps not all, of the money came from the sale of stock.

Hughes also owns about $20 million worth of real estate at Tucson and Phoenix, and about $125 million worth at Culver City, California. And he has a $6-million interest in the Atlas Corp.

Estimates of Hughes's visible assets thus would look like this:

Assets	Conservation Evaluation	Liberal Evaluation
Hughes Aircraft Co.	$187,500,000	$375,000,000
Hughes Tool Co. (excluding outside investments)	200,000,000	300,000,000
Real estate	245,000,000	245,000,000
Remaining from stock sales	347,000,000	447,000,000
Atlas Corp. stock	6,000,000	6,000,000
Total	$985,500,000	$1,373,000,000

By both a conservative and a liberal evaluation, Hughes shows a slim margin over Getty when only visible assets are considered. But both may have other assets, for example cash and securities, which remain invisible. Because of this, and because of all the other imponderables, Getty and Hughes must be declared tied for the title of Richest American.

The Social Background of Political Decision-Makers

Donald R. Matthews

Social Class and Political Recruitment

The mythology of American politics is heavily influenced by a log cabin to White House motif. Despite the growing evidence of class distinctions in American society, the notion persists that politics is one area of life in which the American dream can come true. The theories analyzed . . . however, suggest that this view is unrealistic. Regardless of democratic institutions and values, political decision-makers will tend to be chosen from among those ranking high in America's system of social stratification. Which view is correct? When the scattered studies of American political personnel are drawn together, they supply us with a reasonably trustworthy answer to this question.

Father's Occupation

Probably the most important single criterion for social ranking in the United States is occupation. Although it is by no means a certain index to an individual's social standing in the community, occupation is perhaps the closest approach to an infallible guide. Thus information on the occupations of the fathers of American political decision-makers provides a reasonably accurate picture of their class origins. As is plainly evident in Table 1, those American political decision-makers *for whom this information is available* are, with very few exceptions, sons of professional men, proprietors and officials, and farmers. A very small minority were sons of wage earners, low-salaried workers, farm laborers or servants. When this fact is compared with the occupational distribution of the labor force in 1890, the narrow base from which political decision-makers appear to be recruited is clear.

Table 1.   Occupational Class of Fathers of American Political Decision-Makers (In Percentages)

Occupational Class of Father	President, Vice-president, Cabinet 1789–1934	High Level Civil Servant 1940	U.S. Senators 81st Congress 1949–51	U.S. Representatives** 77th Congress 1941–43	Labor Force 1890
Professional	38	28	22	31	5
Proprietors & officials	20	30	33	31	6
Farmers	38	29	40	29	26
Low salaried workers	*	3	1	0	5
Wage earners	4	10	3	9	36
Servants	0	0	0	0	7
Farm laborers	0	0	0	0	15
Unknown, unclassified	0	0	1	0	0
	100	100	100	100	100
	(n=311)	(n=180)	(n=109)	(n=186)	

*Less than 1.
**Subject to substantial error because of incomplete data.

If this were all the evidence available, conclusions about the relationship between social stratification and political life chances would have to be extremely tentative. Fortunately a great deal of other relevant data exists. . . .

All of the facts presented so far in this section suggest that the log cabin to White House myth is rather far from the truth. For the most part political decision-makers are far from common men in either their origins or their achievements. This conclusion is greatly strengthened by the facts about their occupational backgrounds.

The results of a number of efforts to determine the occupational levels of recent political decision-makers are presented in Table 7. According to these studies, about 90% of each group in the table are drawn from the top 15% or so of the labor force. However as the importance of the public office declines, we find a gradual decline in the occupational status of its usual incumbent. Thus, for example, the state legislatures appear to be far more "democratic" in composition than the Congress of the United States or the state governorships. Moreover while empirical studies of historical trends in the occupational distribution of political decision-makers are scarce, the evidence that does exist suggests that their occupational level has not changed a great deal during the last century and a half.

Table 2.   Educational Level of American Political Decision-Makers
(In Percentages)

Highest Level Attained	Presidents, Vice-presidents, Cabinet Members (1877-1934)	Supreme Court Justices (1897-1937)	United States Senators (1949-51)	United States Representatives (1941-43)
None	0	0	0	0
Grade school	11	0	3	0
High school	10	0	10	12
College	79	100	87	88
	100	100	100	100
	(n=176)	(n=20)	(n=108)	(n=431)

Highest Level Attained	High-Level Civil Servants (1940)	State Governors (1930-40)	Missouri State Legislators (1901-31)	Population Over 25 Years of Age (1940)
None	0	0	0	5
Grade school	0	3	30	54
High school	7	20	13	31
College	93	77	57	10
	100	100	100	100
	(n=242)	(n=135)	(n=2,876)	

Table 3. Occupational Class of American Political Decision-Makers
(In Percentages)

Occupational Class	President, Vice-president, Cabinet* 1877-1934	United States Senators 1949-51	United States Representatives 1949-51	State Governors 1930-40	State Legislators** 1925-35	Labor Force 1940
Professionals	74	69	69	60	36	7
Lawyers	70 ⎫	57 ⎫	56 ⎫	52 ⎫	28 ⎫	
Others	4 ⎭	12 ⎭	13 ⎭	8 ⎭	8 ⎭	
Proprietors & officials	21	24	22	25	25	8
Farmers	2	7	4	11	22	11
Low-salaried workers	1	0	1	1	4	17
Wage earners	2	0	2	1	3	40
Servants	0	0	0	0	0	11
Farm laborers	0	0	0	0	0	7
Unknown, unclassified	0	0	2	3	10	0
	100 (n=176)	100 (n=109)	100 (n=435)	101 (n=170)	100 (n=12,689)	101

*Occupations in this column are those for which presidents, vice-presidents, and cabinet officers were trained.
**Figures for the lower houses of 13 selected states and the upper houses of 12. The states are Arkansas, California (lower house only), Illinois, Indiana, Iowa, Louisiana, Maine, Minnesota, Mississippi, New Jersey, New York, Pennsylvania, Washington.

Lawyers: High Priests of American Politics

One small occupational group, the legal profession, has supplied a large majority of America's top-level public officials throughout our entire history. Twenty-five of the 52 signers of the Declaration of Independence were lawyers, 31 of the 55 members of the Continental Congress, 23 out of the 33 men who have served as President of the United States have been lawyers. Another look at Table 3 will indicate that the legal profession, comprising about one-tenth of one per cent of the labor force, still supplies a majority of American decision-makers. Why this predominance of lawyers?

Lawyers meet what seems to be the first prerequisite of top-level political leadership: they are in a high-prestige occupation. But so are physicians, businessmen, and scientists. Why are lawyers dominant in politics rather than members of these other high-prestige groups? Certainly any attempt to explain the origins and development of American political leaders must be able to account for this.

The answer to these questions can be found in the skills of the lawyer and the nature of the legal profession in America. The skills developed by the lawyer in the practice of his profession give him an advantage in the race for office, if not actual training for the performance of public duties. His job involves skill in interpersonal mediation and conciliation and facility in the use of words. Both of these skills are indispensable to the politician. Moreover the lawyer in private practice operates in large part as the expert adviser to decision-makers. As Lasswell and McDougal put it:

> ...the lawyer is to-day...the one indispensable adviser of every responsible policy-maker of our society—whether we speak of the head of a government department or agency, of the executive of a corporation or labor union, of the secretary of a trade or other private association, or even of the humble independent enterpriser or professional man. As such an adviser the lawyer, when informing his policy-maker of what he can or cannot legally do, is in an unassailably strategic position to influence, if not create, policy.... For better or worse our decision-makers and our lawyers are bound together in a relation of dependence or of identity.

With the development of these skills in the normal course of an occupational career, the lawyer is at a substantial advantage over the average layman who decides to enter politics.

The position of the legal profession in American society must be considered as another factor contributing to the lawyers' political dominance. Unlike many other countries the United States has never had a landed aristocracy with a tradition of public service. While most political decision-makers enjoy high-prestige positions, few are the possessors of inherited wealth. In a highly competitive society in which occupational success is the most highly valued goal for the ambitious, who can with the least danger leave their jobs for the tremendous risks of a political career? Among the high-prestige occupations the answer seems to be the lawyers. Certainly other professionals find the neglect of their careers for political activities extremely hazardous. In the professions in which the subject matter is changing rapidly, such as medicine, science, and engineering, with a few years of neglect special skills are either lost or become outmoded. The active businessman, either an individual entrepreneur or a member of a corporate bureaucracy, usually finds neglect of his vocation for politics no asset to his primary occupational interest. Politics is demanding more and more time from its practitioners. A man who actively manages a farm finds it difficult to indulge a taste for politics under these conditions.

These barriers to sustained political activity either do not exist or are decreased in significance for the lawyer. For the most part the law changes relatively slowly, and a lawyer-politician is usually in a position to keep up with such changes while active in politics. The lawyer who typically is in solo practice or a member of a small law firm is dispensable. He can easily combine his occupation on a part-time basis with political activity. This activity may be an actual advantage to his occupational advancement. Free and professionally legitimate advertising, contacts, and opportunities to meet other (often important) lawyers of his area result from his political activities, to say nothing of possible appointments to judicial office. Thus a lawyer entering political life does not cut himself off from the possibilities of occupational success; indeed he may actually enhance such prospects. This is not the case for other high-prestige occupations.

Thus the facts about the occupational backgrounds of American political decision-makers indicate that more than high social status is necessary in order to have high political opportunities. Some positions of high social status may actually be a detriment to the politically ambitious. But where high prestige is combined with training in interpersonal relations, easy access to politics, and "dispensability," as is the case for the lawyers, the result is a dominant position in American politics.

Is There a Ruling Class in the United States?

After this brief review of some of the findings of empirical studies of American political decision-makers, we are in a position to answer the question with which we began: is there a ruling class in the United States?

Certainly not as the elite and ruling-class theorists use the term! We have found that the public officials who make the most important political decisions in the United States are a fairly heterogeneous lot. There are substantial differences in their origins and experiences. It is also evident that the avenues to positions of political power are not completely closed even to relatively low-status groups such as Negroes, immigrants, and the poorly educated. But this same evidence shows that political opportunities tend to be best for those in positions near the top of the American class system and worst for those near the bottom. As a result our political decision-makers, taken as a whole, are very far from being a cross section of the electorate. Rather there seems to be a sort of class ranking of public offices in the United States—the more important the office, the higher the social status of its normal incumbent. Thus incumbents in the top offices are mostly upper- and upper-middle-class people.

It would be a mistake to attribute this fact to any kind of conscious plot. Such a point of view is hardly justified. What seems to happen in the United States is far simpler than this. First, there is the obvious fact that the money and time necessary for sustained political activity are possessed by only a minority of the American people. The higher up the social scale an individual is, the more likely he is to possess these prerequisites, although even some high-prestige groups do not have both. Second, opportunities to obtain the requisite status, time, and money are far from equal. Studies of stratification in America show with monotonous regularity that a head start helps in the race for social success. The same is true of one's chances for obtaining advanced education and professional skills. Finally it seems understandable in a society with an accepted stratification system for the electorate to choose men with high social status to represent them in the decision-making process. A man with a fairly high social position has met the society's definition of success. Rightly or wrongly the lawyer is thought to be a better man than the factory worker. Thus when the factory worker votes for the lawyer he is voting for a man who is what he would *like* to be. All of these factors and perhaps even more are involved in explaining the impact of social class on the nature of America's top-level political personnel.

Another warning is in order. It is misleading to assume that a group must literally be represented among the political decision-makers to have influence or political power. The unrepresentative nature of America's political decision-makers no doubt has its consequences, but it does not free them from their ultimate accountability to the electorate at large. Thus the frequency with which members of certain groups are found among decision-makers should not be considered an infallible index of the distribution of power in a society. In America at least lower-status groups have political power far in excess of their number in Congress, the Cabinet, and so on. And there seems to be some evidence that those at the very apex of the social hierarchy are also represented not literally but by sympathetic agents such as lawyers and professional politicians.

The Modern Corporation and the State
John Galbraith

The industrial system, in fact, is inextricably associated with the state. In notable respects the mature corporation is an arm of the state. And the state, in important matters, is an instrument of the industrial system. This runs strongly counter to the accepted doctrine. That assumes and affirms a clear line between government and private business enterprise. The position of this line—what is given to the state and what is accorded to private enterprise—tells whether the society is socialist or non-socialist. Nothing is so important. Any union between public and private organization is held, by liberal and conservative alike, to be deviant sin. To the liberal it means that public power has been captured for private advantage and profit. To the conservative it means that high private prerogative has been lost to the state. In fact, the line between public and private authority in the industrial system is indistinct and in large measure imaginary, and the abhorrent association of public and private organizations is normal. When this is perceived, the central trends in American economic and political life become clear. On few matters is an effort to free the mind more rewarding.

Members of the technostructure, we have seen, identify themselves with its goals because they find these goals superior to their own and because there is a chance of adapting them to their own. The relationship of the technostructure of the mature corporation to the state is the same. The state is strongly concerned with the stability of the economy. And with its expansion or growth. And with education. And with technical and scientific advance. And, most notably, with the national defense. These are *the* national goals; they are sufficiently trite so that one has a reassuring sense of the obvious in articulating them. All have their counterpart in the needs and goals of the technostructure. It requires stability in demand for its planning. Growth brings promotion and prestige. It requires trained manpower. It needs government underwriting of research and development. Military and other technical procurement support its most developed form of planning. At each point the government has goals with which the technostructure can identify itself. Or, plausibly, these goals reflect adaptation of public goals to the goals of the technostructure. As the individual serves the technostructure in response to a complex system of motivation in which identification and adaptation are extremely important, so the same motivation is reflected in the relations of the mature corporation to the state. Again we find the principle of consistency rendering faithful service. Therein lies the influence of the mature corporation—an influence which makes purely pecuniary relationships pallid by comparison.

Let us now give these abstractions specific form—and put them to test.

The practical manifestation of this process is to be seen most clearly in defense procurement. With the $60 billion it spends for this purpose each year (as this is written) the Department of Defense supports, as noted, the most highly developed planning in the industrial system. It provides contracts of long duration, calling for large investment of capital in areas of advanced technology. There is no risk of price fluctuations. There is full protection against any change in requirements, i.e., any change in demand. Should a contract be canceled the firm is protected on the investment it has made. For no other products can the technostructure plan with such certainty and assurance. Given the inevitability of planning, there is much attraction in circumstances where it can be done so well.

This leads the technostructure to identify itself closely with the goals of the armed services and, not infrequently, with the specific goals of the particular service, Army, Navy or Air Force, which it most intimately serves. Simple association, as in the case of individual and organization, supports this tendency. In consequence the technostructure comes to see the same urgency in weapons development, the same security in technical pre-eminence, the same requirement for a particular weapons system, the same advantage in an enlarged mission for (say) the Air Force or Navy, as does the particular service itself. Its members develop the same commitment to these goals as do officers of the services.

This relationship accords parallel opportunity for adaptation. The need to combine the work of diverse specialists and technicians means that the development of (say) a new weapons system requires organization. This the technostructure, and frequently it alone, can provide. So the armed services are deeply dependent on their supplying corporations for technical development. And, in practice, numerous other tasks requiring the resources of organization—the planning of logistics systems, planning and development of base facilities, even on occasion the definitions of the missions of a particular service or one of its branches—are contracted out to supplying corporations. "In its rapid climb during the fifties, the Air Force fostered a growing band of private companies which took over a substantial part of regular military operations, including maintaining aircraft, firing rockets, building and maintaining launching sites, organizing and directing other contractors, and making major public decisions. ... The Air Force's success over her sister services ... established the magic formula that all federal agencies soon imitated."

A firm that is developing a new generation of fighter aircraft is in an admirable position to influence the design and equipment of the plane. It can have something to say on the mission for which it is adapted, the number of planes required, their deployment, and, by implication, on the choice of the enemy toward which it is directed. This will reflect the firm's own views, and, *pari passu,* its own needs. If the firm has been accorded a more explicit planning function, it helps to establish assumptions as to probable enemies, points of probable attack, the nature of the resulting hostilities and the other factors on which defense procurement depends. In conjunction with other such planning, including, of course, that of public agencies, it helps to establish the official view of defense requirements and therewith of some part of the foreign policy. These will be a broad reflection of the firm's own goals; it would be eccentric to expect otherwise.

This influence is not absolute. In the autumn of 1962, the Department of Defense canceled plans for further development of the Skybolt, a missile of disturbingly erratic behavior designed for launching in flight from a manned bomber. If successful, it would have insured, in turn, a further demand for manned bombers, a weapon which otherwise would be obsolescent. In advertising and other forms of persuasion, the putative manufacturer made a strong case for the eventual technical proficiency of Skybolt and its importance in the defensive strategy of the United States. It failed. But the failure was not in this last rather desperate effort but in the earlier inability to have it incorporated, without particular public discussion, in the general catalog of military needs. This would have been the normal manifestation of influence. . . .

Identification and adaptation cannot ordinarily be reconciled with political hostility to the state or any particular party or administration. As noted, the entrepreneurial corporation did not have an intimate and continuing dependence on the state; its fortunes in respect of the state were affected by individual and discreet actions—the award of a contract, sale of public lands, imposition of a tax or tariff, passage of a regulation—which it could influence as such without worrying excessively about the general political environment. But the mature corporation has a continuing and intimate relationship for which doors must always be open and access to public officials always be easy and without tension. Adverse political action or even hostile oratory lessens this ease of access. Men arriving with the briefcases for the day's meetings in Washington or at Wright Field cannot have the added burden of explaining the testimony of a company president who has just attacked the government and all its minions hip and thigh.

But this is not a mere matter of expediency. Identification is a psychological phenomenon. If it is operative, there can be no mental or moral barriers to accepting the goals of the state. Such will be the consequence of political polemics and conflict. To denounce Democrats as destroyers of business and liberal Republicans as conscious agents of Communism is to proclaim one's alienation from their goals. For the technostructure it means rejecting the identification and therewith the adaptation which are the source of its power. This, obviously, makes no sense.

We have here a guide to the political tendencies of the modern large corporation. Increasingly it will be passive rather than active in politics. It will eschew any strong identification with a political party—as the entrepreneur is identified with the Republican Party. It will not speak out on partisan issues. To some extent, perhaps, it will take on the political coloration of whatever party is in office.

All of this is by way of protecting a much stronger and more vital position of influence as an extension of the arm of the bureaucracy. In this role the corporation can participate in the decisions that count. It can help shape the highly technical choices which, in turn, govern the demand for its own military and other products. It will have access to the decisions on military strategy which establish the need for such products. And it will help to shape the current beliefs or assumptions on foreign policy. These, obviously, are a far more important power. It is the difference between the formal grandeur of the legislative hearing and the shirt-sleeved rooms with blackboards and tables heavy with data, drawings and tapes where the important decisions, bit by bit, are actually made. The technostructure selects its theater of influence with discrimination and intelligence.

Professionals in Violence
Morris Janowitz

Five Basic Hypotheses

Five working hypotheses supply the point of departure for an analysis of the military profession over the last fifty years, for to speak of the modern military in the United States is to speak of the last half century. These working hypotheses were designed, in particular, for an understanding of the changes that have occurred in the political behavior of the American military. But the American military profession can be adequately understood only by comparison with the military profession of other nation states. The working hypotheses must be applied to the military establishments of other major Western industrialized nations as well. Comparisons between American military establishments and those in Great Britain and Germany, where the military has displayed notable differences in political behavior, are particularly appropriate.

To investigate these hypotheses, direct empirical research was required. Beyond reliance on historical and documentary sources, the social backgrounds and life careers of more than 760 generals and admirals appointed since 1910 were studied; opinion data were collected by means of a questionnaire administered to approximately 550 staff officers on duty in the Pentagon; and 113 officers were intensively interviewed as to their career and ideology.

(1) *Changing organizational authority.* There has been a change in the basis of authority and discipline in the military establishment, a shift from authoritarian domination to greater reliance on manipulation, persuasion, and group consensus. The organizational revolution which pervades contemporary society, and which implies management by means of persuasion, explanation and expertise, is also to be found in the military.

It is common to point out that military organization is rigidly stratified and authoritarian because of the necessities of command and the possibilities of war. The management of war is a serious and deadly business. It is therefore asserted that effective military command permits little tolerance for informal administration. Moreover, because military routines tend to become highly standardized, it is assumed that promotion is in good measure linked to compliance with existing procedures. These characteristics are found in civilian bureaucracies, but supposedly not to the same extent and rigidity. Once an individual has entered the military establishment, he has embarked on a career within a single comprehensive institution. Short of withdrawal, he thereby loses the "freedom of action" that is associated with occupational change in civilian life.

The hypothesis concerning the shift in organizational authority, however, is designed to elucidate the realities of military command, since these realities condition the political behavior of the military elite. It is true that a large segment of the military establishment resembles a civilian bureaucracy insofar as it deals with the problems of research, development, and logistics. Yet, this hypothesis should apply even in areas of the military establishment which are primarily concerned with combat or the maintenance of combat readiness. In fact, the central concern of commanders is no longer the enforcement of rigid discipline, but rather the maintenance of high levels of initiative and morale.

It is in this crucial respect that the military establishment has undergone a slow and continuing change. The technical character of modern warfare requires highly skilled and highly motivated soldiers. In any complex military team an important element of power resides in each member who must make a technical contribution to the success of the undertaking. Therefore, the more mechanized the military formation, the greater the reliance on the team concept of organization.

What dilemmas does this shift in authority pose for an organization with traditions of authoritarian discipline and conservative outlook? If the organizing principle of authority is domination—the issuing of direct commands without giving the reason why—the image of the professional officer is that of the disciplinarian. What are the consequences for the political perspectives of traditional military leaders, if they must operate under this new type of organizational authority?

(2) *Narrowing skill differential between military and civilian elites.* The new tasks of the military require that the professional officer develop more and more of the skills and orientations common to civilian administrators and civilian leaders. The narrowing difference in skill between military and civilian society is an outgrowth of the increasing concentration of technical specialists in the military. The men who perform such technical tasks have direct civilian equivalents: engineers, machine maintenance specialists, health service experts, logistic and personnel technicians. In fact, the concentration of personnel with "purely" military occupational specialties has fallen from 93.2 per cent in the Civil War to 28.8 per cent in the post-Korean Army, and to even lower percentages in the Navy and Air Force.

More relevant to the social and political behavior of the military elite is the required transformation in the skills of the military commander. This hypothesis implies that in order to accomplish his duties, the military commander must become more interested and more skilled in techniques of organization, in the management of morale and negotiation. This is forced on him by the requirements of maintaining initiative in combat units, as well as the necessity of coordinating the ever-increasing number of technical specialists.

Furthermore, the military commander must develop more political orientation, in order to explain the goals of military activities to his staff and subordinates. He must develop a capacity for public relations, in order to explain and relate his organization to other military organizations, to civilian leadership, and to the public. This is not to imply that such skills are found among all top military professionals. Specific types of career lines seem to condition these broad managerial orientations, but the concentration of such skills at the top echelon of the military hierarchy is great, and seems to be growing. As a result, along with a narrowing skill differential between military and civilian elites, transferability of skills from the military establishment to civilian organization has increased.

(3) *Shift in officer recruitment.* The military elite has been undergoing a basic social transformation since the turn of the century. These elites have been shifting their recruitment from a narrow, relatively high, social status base to a broader base, more representative of the population as a whole.

This broadening of the base of recruitment reflects the growth of the military establishment and the demand for larger numbers of trained specialists. In Western Europe, as skill became the basis of recruitment and advancement, the aristocratic monopoly over the officer corps was diminished. In the United States an equivalent process can be demonstrated, although historically, social lines have been more fluid. The Air Force, with its increased demand for technical skill and great expansion over a very short period of time, has offered the greatest opportunity for rapid advancement.

The question can be raised as to whether the broadening social base of recruitment of military leaders is necessarily accompanied by "democratization" of outlook and behavior. One aspect of "democratization" of outlook and behavior implies an increased willingness to be accountable to civilian authority. On the basis of European experiences, particularly in pre-Nazi Germany, there is reason to believe that "democratization" of entrance into the military profession can carry with it potential tendencies to weaken the "democratization" of outlook and behavior.

Are the newer strata in the American military establishment less influenced by the traditions of democratic political control? As the officer corps becomes more socially representative and more heterogeneous, has it become more difficult to maintain organizational effectiveness, and at the same time enforce civilian political control? And, finally, what does representative social recruitment imply for the prestige of the military? Historically, the officer's social prestige was regulated by his family origin and by an ethos which prized heroism and service to the state. What society at large thought of him was of little importance, as long as his immediate circle recognized his calling. This was particularly true of the British officer corps with its aristocratic and landed-gentry background and its respectable middle-class service families.

But, as the military profession grows larger and socially more heterogeneous, as it becomes more of a career, does not pressure develop for prestige recognition by the public at large? Every professional soldier, like every businessman or government official, represents his establishment and must work to enhance the prestige of his profession. In turn, a military figure can become a device for enhancing a civilian enterprise. Do not such trends force the military to become more obtrusive and place a strain on traditional patterns of civilian-military relations?

(4) *Significance of career patterns.* Prescribed careers performed with high competence lead to entrance into the professional elite, the highest point in the military hierarchy at which technical and routinized functions are performed. By contrast, entrance into the smaller group—the elite nucleus—where innovating perspectives, discretionary responsibility, and political skills are required is assigned to persons with unconventional and adaptive careers.

This hypothesis is probably applicable to all organizations, for top leadership, especially in a crisis, is seldom reserved for those who take no risks. But among the military the belief in a prescribed career is particularly strong. An unconventional career, within limits, can imply a predisposition toward innovation, or, at least, criticism of the operation of the military establishment at any given moment. It implies that the officer has undergone experiences which have enabled him to acquire new perspectives, new skills, and a broader outlook than is afforded by a routine career. Unconventional or unusual careers, however, must be developed within the framework of existing institutions, since officers who express too openly their desire to innovate or to criticize are not likely to survive.

All types of elites must be skilled in managing interpersonal relations, in making strategic decisions, and in political negotiations, rather than in the performance of technical tasks. Yet, they enter these leadership roles through prescribed careers which emphasize technical tasks. If this is a correct hypothesis, then the study of career development in the armed forces should throw some light on the process by which a minority of military leaders departed from their prescribed careers to become concerned with broader military issues, and with the social and political consequences of violence in international relations.

(5) *Trends in political indoctrination.* The growth of the military establishment into a vast managerial enterprise with increased political responsibilities has produced a strain on traditional military self-images and concepts of honor. The officer is less and less prepared to think of himself as merely a military technician. As a result, the profession, especially within its strategic leadership, has developed a more explicit political ethos. Politics, in this sense, has two meanings; one internal, the other external. On the internal level politics involves the activities of the military establishment in influencing legislative and administrative decisions regarding national security policies and affairs. On the external level politics encompasses the consequences of military actions on the international balance of power and the behavior of foreign states. The two aspects of military "politics" are, of course, intertwined.

Since the outbreak of World War II, career experiences and military indoctrination at all levels have resulted in much broader perspectives—social and political—than had been the tradition. Yet, what the consequences are likely to be for civil-military relations in a democratic society is very much an open question. It may well be that these experiences have had the effect of making the military profession more critical of, and more negative toward, civilian political leadership.

In particular, prevailing patterns of belief in the armed forces require careful examination. It is clear that in the United States current indoctrination in the armed forces is designed to eliminate the civilian contempt for the "military mind." The "military mind" has been charged with traditionalism and with a lack of inventiveness. The new doctrine stresses initiative and continuous innovation. The "military mind" has been charged with an inclination toward ultra-nationalism and ethnocentrism. Military professionals are being taught to de-emphasize ethnocentric thinking, since ethnocentrism is counter to national and military policy. The "military mind" has been charged with being disciplinarian. The new doctrine seeks to deal with human factors in combat and large-scale organization in a manner conforming to contemporary thought on human relations. In short, the new indoctrination seems to be designed to supply the military professional with opinions on many political, social, and economic subjects, opinions which he feels obliged to form as a result of his new role, and to which he was expected to be indifferent in the past.

Much of this indoctrination is designed to develop a critical capacity and a critical orientation. Will the growth of critical capacities be destructive of professional loyalties, or will it be productive of new solutions? Will the present increased effort to politicize the military profession produce negative attitudes? In the United States any such hostility is hardly likely to lead to open disaffection; it is more apt to cause quiet resentment and bitterness.

These hypotheses are designed to contribute answers to questions which focus primarily on politics and policy: How can the past political behavior of the military in the conduct of war and in domestic politics be explained? How adequate and well prepared are top military leaders for the continuing political tasks which must of necessity be performed by the military establishment?

Three issues are central in evaluating the political behavior of the military profession. First, in the past the military profession has been considered deficient in its ability to judge the political consequences of its conduct. The American military have been criticized for their lack of political sensitivity in directing and executing military tasks. Some of the sharpest criticism has come from military statesmen themselves. General Omar Bradley, in his memoirs, stated with considerable detachment, "At times, during the war, we forgot that wars are fought for the resolution of political conflicts, and in the ground campaign for Europe, we sometimes overlooked political considerations of vast importance." In a deeper sense, the behavior of the American military was not so much unpolitical, as inappropriate and inadequate for the requirements of a world-wide system of security. The growth of the destructive power of warfare increases, rather than decreases, the political involvements and responsibilities of the military. The solution to international relations becomes less and less attainable by use of force, and each strategic and tactical decision is not merely a matter of military administration, but an index of political intentions and goals.

Second, somewhat paradoxically, the military have been charged with exceeding their proper role in a political democracy. The military profession is criticized as carrying too much weight and influence in the formulation of foreign policy, especially by overemphasizing the function of violence. As compared with that of Great Britain, our military force seems much too active and outspoken as a legislative pressure group and as a "public relations" force. Even a sympathetic military commentator, Hanson W. Baldwin, has asserted: "The influence of the military on public opinion—a necessary influence in the atomic age— has reached the point today where it is time to call a halt."

The greater economic and human resources of the military establishment and its increased responsibility result in greater domestic political involvement. But to what extent does this expansion represent a response to a vacuum created by the ineffectiveness of civilian institutions and leaders? It cannot be assumed that such expansion represents "designed militarism." Designed militarism—the type identified with Prussian militarism—develops from lack of effective traditions for controlling the military establishment, as well as from a failure of civilian leaders to act relevantly and consistently. Under such circumstances, a vacuum is created which not only encourages an extension of the power of military leadership, but actually compels such trends. Unanticipated militarism seems more likely to account for crucial aspects of contemporary problems in the United States.

Third, in the past the military profession has been judged deficient because of its social and intellectual isolation from civilian society. While the extent of this segregation is probably exaggerated, it is clear that before World War II this exclusiveness helped the profession to maintain its *esprit de corps*, and to retain its officer personnel during a period of civilian indifference. Contrary to popular belief, the resignation rate for academy graduates from the armed forces during the inter-war years was very low. However, if since World War II the military profession has abandoned its social isolation, it has also experienced an increased exodus of younger officers, including academy graduates. By military standards, the rate is considered high.

In 1957 official studies reported a shortage of 28 percent of younger officers in the 4–14 year service group. A study of Army lieutenants concluded that officers with higher potentiality for advancement tended to resign after completing their obligatory service, while those who were less qualified remained. To date, the lack of sufficiently qualified new junior officers has been compensated by substantial resources of trained and experienced officers carried over from World War II. By 1963, however, many of these officers, having completed twenty years of service, will end their active duty. In the meantime this trend in resignations of academy graduates has increased since 1951 to the level where one out of every four or five academy graduates leaves the service within five years after being commissioned. Any evaluation of the military profession involves its ability to attract and retain superior personnel, a baffling problem in a political democracy, where the professional soldier holds an ambiguous position.

As a result of the complex machinery of warfare, which has weakened the line between military and non-military organization, the military establishment has come more and more to display the characteristics typical of any large-scale organization. Nevertheless, the military establishment creates its special environment and influences its decision-making process. Social background, military authority, and career experiences condition the perspectives of its leaders. The style of life of the military community and a sense of military honor serve to perpetuate professional distinctiveness. Recognition of the specialized attributes of the military profession will provide a realistic basis for maintaining civilian political supremacy without destroying required professional autonomy.

But the military have not emerged as a leadership group with a unified theory of war and a consistent set of tactics for influencing executive and legislative decisions. On the contrary, military leaders are sharply divided on issues of military strategy and the necessities of national security. The analysis of the military as a professional group should throw light on the career experiences and personal alliances which are at the root of these differing concepts of military doctrine.

Bibliography

Stanley Lieberson, "An Empirical Study of Military-Industrial Linkages," *American Journal of Sociology*, 71 (Jan. 1971), pp. 562-584. Neither elitist nor pluralist explanations are adequate to account for excessive military spending.

Edwin M. Epstein, *The Corporation in American Politics* (Englewood Cliffs: Prentice-Hall, Inc., 1969). A refutation of the corporate elite theories of C. Wright Mills.

Morton S. Baratz, "Corporate Giants and the Power Structure," *Western Political Quarterly*, IIX (June, 1956), pp. 406-415. A somewhat dated, but theoretically elegant argument on the central role of corporate wealth in the generation of political power.

Herbert Jacob, "Initial Recruitment of Elected Officials in the U.S.—A Model," *Journal of Politics*, 24 (Nov. 1962), pp. 703-716. Jacob's thesis is that elected officials have "broker" type personality characteristics and hence come primarily from "brokerage" occupations.

Samuel P. Huntington, *The Soldier and the State* (New York: Vintage Books, 1964). Huntington considers the degree to which civilian control of the military is feasible and desirable.

James Q. Wilson and Edward C. Banfield, "Public-Regardingness as a Value Premise in Voting Behavior," *American Political Science Review*, LVIII (Dec. 1964), pp. 576-887. Banfield and Wilson stress the fact that upper income groups often vote against their economic self interest.

The Many Who Do Not:

Masses In America

Elites and masses differ not only in socio-economic background and control of societal resources, but also in attitudes and values. Elites give greater support than masses to the principles and beliefs underlying the political system. Elitism includes the following notions about mass behavior:

(1) Elites give greater support to democratic values than masses. The masses will respond positively to abstract democratic symbols because they have been taught to do so, but they are frequently unwilling to apply general principles to specific individuals, groups, or events.

(2) Intolerant extremist movements in modern society are more likely to find support in the lower classes than in the middle and upper classes. Such mass movements exploit alienation and hostility by concentrating upon "scapegoats."

(3) The masses are less committed to democratic rules of the game than elites. Mass political activism tends to be undemocratic, unstable, and frequently violent.

(4) Given the undemocratic sentiments of the masses, their usual political apathy and nonparticipation actually contributes to the survival of democratic values. Only an unusual demagogue or crisis situation can arouse the masses from their apathy and create a threat to the established system.

(5) Elite-mass communication is very difficult. The masses are ignorant about most political issues and consequently cannot convey any lucid message to decision makers.

(6) Democracy does not survive because of broad support among the masses, but rather because of the elite commitment to democratic ideals.

Modern evidence from the social sciences is conclusive on at least one point: elites give greater support to democratic values than masses. Herbert McCloskey's interesting work, "Consensus and Ideology in American Politics," represents many other studies which document the differing commitment of elites and masses to democratic values—tolerance, freedom of speech and press, due process of law, faith in democracy, political equality, and human dignity. McCloskey's operational definition of "political influentials" is distilled from the study of delegates and alternates to Democratic and Republican national conventions. These individuals are certainly not in America's *top* governing elite, as that term is commonly understood in elite theory; yet (according to McCloskey) even these relatively minor party functionaries show, when compared with ordinary voters, a more developed sense of democratic ideology and a firmer grasp of its essentials. They approve democratic ideas more strongly, tend to tolerate proper procedures and citizen rights, better understand and accept "rules of the game," and affirm the political system more consistently. McCloskey himself does not place his findings in the theoretical framework of elitism, but he is aware that they do not conform to traditional democratic and pluralist assumptions. In his conclusion, he takes comfort from the fact that the masses are generally apathetic about politics and the fact that they do not act upon their antidemocratic values.

Seymour Martin Lipset's essay on "Working Class Authoritarianism" is drawn from his influential book *Political Man*. Here Lipset documents the general authoritarian character of working class populations, and more importantly, provides an explanation for their authoritarianism based upon research into childhood experiences, family relationships, educational attainment, cultural opportunities, job experiences, and social isolation. Here again the implication is made that mass apathy is important to the survival of democratic values.

Robert Lane's essay "The Fear of Equality" is drawn from his larger work *Political Ideology*, which delves into the personal and political beliefs of twenty-eight white, middle-class Americans. Professor Lane documents the general quiescence of the masses: their general satisfaction with their lower class status, their belief in inequality, and their disinclination to assume the responsibilities of governing. Lane notes that their inactivity is based upon several things: the fact that they perceive *some* individuals to be lower on the class ladder than themselves; the fact that they can justify inequalities on the basis of educational attainment, their belief that *some* opportunities exist for their upward social movement, and their consciousness of some degree of economic security. It is interesting to speculate whether or not Lane's masses would remain quiet if any of these factors were missing.

Sociologist William Kornhouser in his book *Politics in Mass Society* describes the characteristics of mass political behavior. According to him, mass political behavior is direct, unmediated, undemocratic, violence-prone, unstable, unpredictable, and extremist. Totalitarian movements of both the left and the right are typically movements which express mass feelings of resentment against the present established order. Totalitarian movements, either conservative or radical, have their greatest appeal among alienated and atomized people who have no strong commitments to established groups and organizations.

The Wallace movement typifies mass political movements in America. It is extremist, populist, and intolerant. It appeals to lower class individuals, rural and small town dwellers, and uneducated manual workers, many of whom do not usually vote or belong to organized interest groups. Seymour Martin Lipset and Earl Raab analyze survey data from the 1968 Presidential election in "The Wallace Whitelash" and confirm the populist character of the Wallace candidacy. They also note that over twice as many people sympathized with Wallace as voted for him, suggesting the importance of mass conditioning to the two party system. Finally, they observe that the pattern of Wallace support is essentially the same in both the North and the South, and that Wallace is as strongly supported by youth as by older voters.

Consensus and Ideology in American Politics

Herbert McCloskey

The belief that consensus is a prerequisite of democracy has, since deTocqueville, so often been taken for granted that it is refreshing to find the notion now being challenged. Prothro and Grigg, for example, have questioned whether agreement on "fundamentals" actually exists among the electorate, and have furnished data which indicate that it may not. Dahl, reviewing his study of community decision-makers, has inferred that political stability does not depend upon widespread belief in the superiority of democratic norms and procedures, but only upon their *acceptance*. From the findings turned up by Stouffer, and by Prothro and Grigg, he further conjectures that agreement on democratic norms is greater among the politically active and aware—the "political stratum" as he calls them—than among the voters in general. V. O. Key, going a step further, suggests that the viability of a democracy may depend less upon popular opinion than upon the activities and values of an "aristocratic" strain whose members are set off from the mass by their political influence, their attention to public affairs, and their active role as society's policy makers. "If so, any assessment of the vitality of a democratic system should rest on an examination of the outlook, the sense of purpose, and the beliefs of this sector of society."

Writers who hold consensus to be necessary to a free society have commonly failed to define it precisely or to specify what it must include. Even Tocqueville does not go deeply enough into the matter to satisfy these needs. He tells us that a society can exist and, *a fortiori*, prosper only when "the minds of all the citizens [are] rallied and held together by certain predominant ideas; . . . when a great number of men consider a great number of things from the same aspect, when they hold the same opinions upon many subjects, and when the same occurrences suggest the same thoughts and impressions to their minds"—and he follows this pronouncement with a list of general principles he believes Americans hold in common. Elsewhere, he speaks of the "customs" of the American nation (its "habits, opinions, usages, and beliefs") as "the peculiar cause which renders that people able to support a democratic government." But nowhere does he set forth explicitly the nature of the agreement upon which a democratic society presumably depends.

Later commentators have not clarified matters much. Some, like A. Lawrence Lowell, have avoided Tocqueville's emphasis upon shared ideas, customs, and opinions in favor of the less demanding view that popular government requires agreement mainly "in regard to the legitimate character of the ruling authority and its right to decide the questions that arise." Consensus, in this view, becomes merely a synonym for legitimacy. Others speak of consensus as a sense of solidarity or social cohesion arising from a common ethos or heritage, which unites men into a community. Political scientists have most frequently employed the term to designate a state of agreement about the "fundamental values" or "rules of the game" considered essential for constitutional government. Rarely, however, have writers on consensus attempted to state what the fundamentals must include, how extensive the agreement must be, and *who* must agree. Is agreement required among all men or only among certain of them? Among the entire electorate or only those who actively participate in public affairs? Is the same type of consensus essential for all democracies at all times, or is a firmer and more sweeping consensus needed for periods of crisis than for periods of calm, for newer, developing democracies than for older stable ones?

While certain of these questions are beyond the scope of this paper (no one, in any event, has done the systematic historical and comparative research needed to answer them satisfactorily), something might be learned about the relation of ideological consensus to democracy by investigating the subject in at least one major democracy, the United States. In the present paper I wish to explore further some of the questions raised by the writers I have cited and to present research findings on several hypotheses relating to those questions.

Hypotheses and Definitions

We expected the data to furnish support for the following hypotheses, among others:

> That the American electorate is often divided on "fundamental" democratic values and procedural "rules of the game" and that its understanding of politics and of political ideas is in any event too rudimentary at present to speak of ideological "consensus" among its members.
>
> That, as Prothro and Grigg report for their samples, the electorate exhibits greater support for general, abstract statements of democratic belief than for their specific applications.
>
> That the constituent ideas of American democratic ideology are principally held by the more "articulate" segments of the population, including the political influentials; and that people in these ranks will exhibit a more meaningful and far reaching consensus on democratic and constitutional values than will the general population.
>
> That consensus is far from perfect even among the articulate classes, and will be evidenced on political questions more than on economic ones, on procedural rights more than on public policies, and on freedom more than equality.
>
> That whatever increases the level of political articulateness—education, S.E.S., urban residence, intellectuality, political activity, etc.—strengthens consensus and support for American political ideology and institutions.

Whether a word like ideology can properly be employed in the American context depends, in part, on which of its many connotations one chooses to emphasize. Agreement on the meaning of the term is far from universal, but a tendency can be discerned among contemporary writers to regard ideologies as *systems* of belief that are elaborate, integrated, and coherent, that justify the exercise of power, explain and judge historical events, identify political right and wrong, set forth the interconnections (causal and moral) between politics and other spheres of activity, and furnish guides for action. While liberal democracy does not fulfill perfectly the terms of this definition, it comes close enough, in my opinion, to be considered an ideology. The elements of liberal democratic thought are not nearly so vague as they are sometimes made out to be, and their coalescence into a single body of belief is by no means fortuitous. American democratic "ideology" possesses an elaborately defined theory, a body of interrelated assumptions, axioms, and principles, and a set of ideals that serve as guides for action. Its tenets, postulates, sentiments, and values inspired the great revolutions of the seventeenth and eighteenth centuries, and have been repeatedly and explicitly set forth in fundamental documents, such as the Constitution, the Declaration, and the Federalist Papers. They have been restated with remarkable unanimity in the messages of Presidents, in political speeches, in the pronouncements of judges and constitutional commentators, and in the writings of political theorists, historians, and publicists. They are so familiar that we are likely to see them not as a coherent union of ideas and principles embodying a well-defined political tendency, but as a miscellany of slogans and noble sentiments to be trotted out on ceremonial occasions.

Although scholars or Supreme Court justices might argue over fine points of interpretation, they would uniformly recognize as elements of American democratic ideology such concepts as consent, accountability, limited or constitutional government, representation, majority rule, minority rights, the principle of political opposition, freedom of thought, speech, press, and assembly, equality of opportunity, religious toleration, equality before the law, the rights of juridical defense, and individual self-determination over a broad range of personal affairs. How widely such elements of American liberal democracy are approved, by whom and with what measure of understanding, is another question—indeed, it is the central question to be addressed in this paper. But that they form an integrated body of ideas which has become part of the American inheritance seems scarcely open to debate.

The term consensus will be employed in this paper to designate a state of agreement concerning the aforementioned values. It has principally to do with shared beliefs and not with feelings of solidarity, the willingness to live together, to obey the laws, or to accept the existing government as legitimate. Nor does it refer to an abstract or universal state of mind, but to a measurable state of concurrence around values that can be specified. Consensus exists in degree and can be expressed in quantitative form. No one, of course, can say how close one must come to unanimity before consensus is achieved, for the cutting point, as with any continuous variable, is arbitrary. Still, the term in ordinary usage has been reserved for fairly substantial measures of correspondence, and we shall take as a minimal requirement for consensus a level of agreement reaching 75 per cent. This figure, while also arbitrary, recommends itself by being realistically modest (falling as it does midway between a bare majority and unanimity), and by having been designated in this country and elsewhere as the extraordinary majority required for certain constitutional purposes.

Since I shall in subsequent pages frequently (and interchangeably) employ such terms as the "articulate minority," the "political class," the "political elite," the "political influentials," and the "political stratum," I should also clarify what they are intended to signify. I mean them to refer to those people who occupy themselves with public affairs to an unusual degree, such as government officials, elected office holders, active party members, publicists, officers of voluntary associations, and opinion leaders. The terms do not apply to any definable social class in the usual sense, nor to a particular status group or profession. Although the people they designate can be distinguished from other citizens by their activity and concerns, they are in no sense a community, they do not act as a body, and they do not necessarily possess identical or even harmonious interests. "Articulates" or "influentials" can be found scattered throughout the society, at all income levels, in all classes, occupations, ethnic groups, and communities, although some segments of the population will doubtless yield a higher proportion of them than others. I scarcely need to add that the line between the "articulates" and the rest of the population cannot always be sharply drawn, for the qualities that distinguish them vary in form and degree and no single criterion of classification will satisfy every contingency.

The data for the present inquiry have been taken from a national study of political actives and supporters carried out in 1957-58. I have in a previous paper described the procedures of that study in some detail, and will not trouble to repeat that description here. Perhaps it will suffice for present purposes merely to note the following: national surveys were carried out on two separate samples, the first a sample of over 3,000 political "actives" or "leaders" drawn from the delegates and alternates who had attended the Democratic and Republican conventions of 1956; the second a representative national sample of approximately 1,500 adults in the general population drawn by the American Institute of Public Opinion (Gallup Poll). Gallup interviewers also delivered and introduced the questionnaire to all respondents, discussed its contents with them, and furnished both oral and written instructions for its self-administration and completion. (For sample characteristics, see Appendix B.)

The party actives may be considered an especially pure sample of the "political stratum," for every person in the sample has marked himself off from the average citizen by his greater political involvement. Although the general population sample may be regarded as a sample of "inarticulates," to be compared with the sample of leaders, there are within it, of course, many persons who by virtue of education, profession, organizational activities, etc. can be classified as "articulates." We shall for certain purposes consider them in this light in order to provide further tests for our hypotheses.

Both samples received the same questionnaire—a lengthy instrument containing questions on personal background, political experience, values, attitudes, opinions, political and economic orientation, party outlooks, and personality characteristics. Many of the questions were direct inquiries in the standard form, but most were single sentence "items" with which the respondent was compelled to express his agreement or disagreement. While each of these items can stand alone and be regarded in its own right as an indicator of a person's opinions or attitudes, each of them is simultaneously an integral element of one of the 47 "scales" that was expressly fashioned to afford a more refined and reliable assessment of the attitude and personality predispositions of every respondent. Each of the scales (averaging approximately nine items) has been independently validated either by empirical validation procedures employing appropriate criterion groups, or by a modified Guttman reproducibility procedure (supplemented, in some instances, by a "face validity" procedure utilizing item ratings by experts).

Data on the *scale* scores are presented in Table 4 and are to be distinguished from the "percentage agree" scores for *individual items* presented in the remaining tables.

Findings

"Rules of the game" and democratic values. Although the so-called "rules of the game" are often separated from other democratic values, the distinction is to some extent arbitrary. One might, for example, reasonably regard as "rules of the game" many of the norms governing free speech, press, social and political equality, political toleration, and the enforcement of justice. For convenience, nevertheless, we shall treat separately those responses that stand out from the general body of democratic attitudes by their particular emphasis upon fair play, respect for legal procedures, and consideration for the rights of others. A sample of items expressing these values is presented in Table 1.

The responses to these items show plainly that while a majority of the electorate support the "rules of the game," approval of such values is significantly greater and more uniform among the influentials. The latter have achieved consensus (as we have defined it) on eight of the twelve items and near consensus on three of the remaining four items. The electorate, by contrast, does not meet the criterion for consensus on a single item.

Although the *scales* (as distinguished from individual *items*) cannot appropriately be used to measure *consensus*, comparison of the scores on those scales which most nearly embody the "rules of the game" furnishes additional evidence that the political class responds to such norms more favorably than does the electorate. The proportion scoring high on a scale of "faith in direct action" (a scale measuring the inclination to take the law into one's own hands) is 26.1 per cent for the active political minority and 42.5 per cent for the general population. On a scale assessing the willingness to flout the rules of political integrity, the proportions scoring high are 12.2 per cent and 30.6 per cent respectively. On "totalitarianism," a scale measuring the readiness to subordinate the rights of others to the pursuit of some collective political purpose, only 9.7 per cent of the political actives score high compared with 33.8 per cent of the general population.

Table 1.   Political Influentials vs. the Electorate: Response to Items
Expressing "Rules of the Game"*

Items	Political Influentials (N=3020)	General Electorate (N=1484)
	% Agree	
There are times when it almost seems better for the people to take the law into their own hands rather than wait for the machinery of government to act.	13.3	26.9
The majority has the right to abolish minorities if it wants to.	6.8	28.4
We might as well make up our minds that in order to make the world better a lot of innocent people will have to suffer.	27.2	41.6
If congressional committees stuck strictly to the rules and gave every witness his rights, they would never succeed in exposing the many dangerous subversives they have turned up.	24.7	47.4
I don't mind a politician's methods if he manages to get the right things done.	25.6	42.4
Almost any unfairness or brutality may have to be justified when some great purpose is being carried out.	13.3	32.8
Politicians have to cut a few corners if they are going to get anywhere.	29.4	43.2
People ought to be allowed to vote even if they can't do so intelligently.	65.6	47.6
To bring about great changes for the benefit of mankind often requires cruelty and even ruthlessness.	19.4	31.3
Very few politicians have clean records, so why get excited about the mudslinging that sometimes goes on?	14.8	38.1
It is all right to get around the law if you don't actually break it.	21.2	30.2
The true American way of life is disappearing so fast that we may have to use force to save it.	12.8	34.6

*Since respondents were forced to make a choice on each item, the number of omitted or "don't know" responses was, on the average, fewer than one percent, and thus has little influence on the direction or magnitude of the results reported in this and subsequent tables.

These and other results which could be cited support the claim advanced by earlier investigators like Prothro and Grigg, and Hyman and Sheatsley, that a large proportion of the electorate has failed to grasp certain of the underlying ideas and principles on which the American political system rests. Endorsement of these ideas is not unanimous among the political elite either, but is in every instance greater than that exhibited by the masses.

The picture changes somewhat when we turn from "rules of the game" to items which in a broad, general way express belief in freedom of speech and opinion. As can be seen from Table 2, support for these values is remarkably high for both samples. Both groups, in fact, respond so overwhelmingly to abstract statements about freedom that one is tempted to conclude that for these values, at least, a far-reaching consensus has been achieved. These results become even more striking when we consider that the items in the table are not mere clichés but statements which in some instances closely paraphrase the arguments developed in Mill's essay, *On Liberty*. We cannot, therefore, dismiss them as mere responses to familiar, abstract sentiments which commit the respondent to nothing in particular.

Table 2.   Political Influentials vs. the Electorate: Responses to Items Expressing Support for General Statements of Free Speech and Opinion

Items	Political Influentials (N-3020)	General Electorate (N-1484)
	% Agree	
People who hate our way of life should still have a chance to talk and be heard.	86.9	81.8
No matter what a person's political beliefs are, he is entitled to the same legal rights and protections as anyone else.	96.4	94.3
I believe in free speech for all no matter what their views might be.	89.4	88.9
Nobody has a right to tell another person what he should and should not read.	81.4	80.7
You can't really be sure whether an opinion is true or not unless people are free to argue against it.	94.9	90.8
Unless there is freedom for many points of view to be presented, there is little chance that the truth can ever be known.	90.6	85.2
I would not trust any person or group to decide what opinions can be freely expressed and what must be silenced.	79.1	64.6
Freedom of conscience should mean freedom to be an atheist as well as freedom to worship in the church of one's choice.	87.8	77.0

Still, as can readily be discerned from the items in Table 3, previous investigators have been partially correct, at least, in observing that the principles of freedom and democracy are less widely and enthusiastically favored when they are confronted in their specific, or applied, forms. As Dahl remarks, it is a "common tendency of mankind . . . to qualify universals in application while leaving them intact in rhetoric." This observation, of course, also holds for the political articulates, but to a lesser degree. Not only do they exhibit stronger support for democratic values than does the electorate, but they are also more consistent in applying the general principle to the specific instance. The average citizen has greater difficulty appreciating the importance of certain procedural or juridical rights, especially when he believes the country's internal security is at stake.

Table 3. Political Influentials vs. the Electorate: Response to items Expressing Support for Specific Applications of Free Speech and Procedural Rights

Items	Political Influentials (N-3020)	General Electorate (N-1484)
	% Agree	
Freedom does not give anyone the right to teach foreign ideas in our schools.	45.5	56.7
A man oughtn't to be allowed to speak if he doesn't know what he's talking about.	17.3	36.7
A book that contains wrong political views cannot be a good book and does not deserve to be published.	17.9	50.3
When the country is in great danger we may have to force people to testify against themselves even if it violates their rights.	28.5	36.3
No matter what crime a person is accused of, he should never be convicted unless he has been given the right to face and question his accusers.	90.1	88.1
If a person is convicted of a crime by illegal evidence, he should be set free and the evidence thrown out of court.	79.6	66.1
If someone is suspected of treason or other serious crimes, he shouldn't be entitled to be let out on bail.	33.3	68.9
Any person who hides behind the laws when he is questioned about his activities doesn't deserve much consideration.	55.9	75.7
In dealing with dangerous enemies like the Communists, we can't afford to depend on the courts, the laws and their slow and unreliable methods.	7.4	25.5

Findings which underscore and amplify these conclusions are yielded by a comparison of the scale scores. The data presented in Table 4 confirm that the influentials not only register higher scores on all the pro-democratic scales (faith in freedom, faith in democracy, procedural rights, tolerance), but are more likely to reject antidemocratic sentiments as well. Although they are themselves an elite of a sort, they display greater faith in the capacity of the mass of men to govern themselves, they believe more firmly in political equality, and they more often disdain the "extreme" beliefs embodied in the Right Wing, Left Wing, totalitarian, elitist, and authoritarian scales. Their repudiation of anti-democratic attitudes is by no means unanimous either, but their responses are more uniformly democratic than are those expressed by the electorate.

Table 4. Political Influentials vs. the Electorate: Percentages Scoring High and Low on Democratic and Anti-Democratic Attitude Scales*

Scale	Political Influentials (N-3020)	General Electorate (N-1484)	Scale	Political Influentials (N-3020)	General Electorate (N-1484)
	(%s down)			(%s down)	
Faith in Democracy			Elitism		
% High	40.1	18.5	% High	22.8	38.7
% Low	14.4	29.7	% Low	41.0	22.4
Procedural Rights			Totalitarianism		
% High	58.1	24.1	% High	9.7	33.8
% Low	12.3	31.3	% Low	60.1	28.4
Tolerance			Right Wing		
% High	61.3	43.1	% High	17.5	33.1
% Low	16.4	33.2	% Low	45.3	28.9
Faith in Freedom			Left Wing		
% High	63.0	48.4	% High	6.7	27.8
% Low	17.1	28.4	% Low	68.7	39.3
Ethnocentrism			California F-Scale		
% High	27.5	36.5	% High	14.7	33.5
% Low	46.9	36.3	% Low	48.0	23.5

Equalitarian values. If Americans concur most strongly about liberty in the abstract, they disagree most strongly about equality. Examples of equalitarian values are presented in Table 5. Both the political stratum and the public divide sharply on these values, a finding which holds for political, as well as for social and economic equality. Both are torn not only on the empirical question of whether men are *in fact* equal but also on the normative issue of whether they should be *regarded* as equal. Neither comes close to achieving consensus on such questions as the ability of the people to rule themselves, to know their best interests in the long run, to understand the issues, or to pick their own leaders wisely. Support for these equalitarian features of "popular" democracy, however, is greater among the elite than among the masses.

Table 5. Political Influentials vs. the Electorate: Responses to Items Expressing Belief in Equality

Items	Political Influentials (N-3020)	General Electorate (N-1484)
	% Agree	
Political Equality		
The main trouble with democracy is that most people don't really know what's best for them.	40.8	58.0
Few people really know what is in their own best interest in the long run.	42.6	61.1
"Issues" and "arguments" are beyond the understanding of most voters.	37.5	62.3
Most people don't have enough sense to pick their own leaders wisely.	28.0	47.8
It will always be necessary to have a few strong, able people actually running everything.	42.5	56.2
Social and Ethnic Equality		
We have to teach children that all men are created equal but almost everyone knows that some are better than others.	54.7	58.3
Just as is true of fine race horses, some breeds of people are just naturally better than others.	46.0	46.3
Regardless of what some people say, there are certain races in the world that just won't mix with Americans.	37.2	50.4
When it comes to the things that count most, all races are certainly not equal.	45.3	49.0
The trouble with letting certain minority groups into a nice neighborhood is that they gradually give it their own atmosphere.	49.8	57.7
Economic Equality		
Labor does not get its fair share of what it produces.	20.8	44.8
Every person should have a good house, even if the government has to build it for him.	14.9	28.2
I think the government should give a person work if he can't find another job.	23.5	47.3
The government ought to make sure that everyone has a good standard of living.	34.4	55.9
There will always be poverty, so people might as well get used to the idea.	40.4	59.4

The reverse is true for the values of economic equality. Among the political stratum, indeed, the weight of opinion is against equality—a result strongly though not exclusively influenced by the pronounced economic conservatism of the Republican leaders in the sample. Support for economic equality is only slightly greater among the electorate. The pattern, furthermore, is extremely spotty, with some policies strongly favored and others as strongly rejected. Thus approval is widespread for public policies (such as social security) that are designed to overcome gross inequalities, but is equally strong for certain features of economic life that promote inequality, such as private enterprise, economic competition, and unlimited pursuit of profit. On social and ethnic equality, both samples are deeply split.

In short, both the public and its leaders are uncertain and ambivalent about equality. The reason, I suspect, lies partly in the fact that the egalitarian aspects of democratic theory have been less adequately thought through than other aspects, and partly in the complications connected with the concept itself. One such complication arises from the historical association of democracy with capitalism, a commingling of egalitarian and inegalitarian elements that has never been (and perhaps never can be) perfectly reconciled. Another complication lies in the diffuse and variegated nature of the concept, a result of its application to at least four separate domains: political (*e.g.*, universal suffrage), legal (*e.g.*, equality before the law), economic (*e.g.*, equal distribution of property or opportunity), and moral (*e.g.*, every man's right to be treated as an end and not as a means). Accompanying these are the confusions which result from the common failure to distinguish equality as a *fact* from equality as a *norm*. ("All men are created equal," for example, is taken by some as an empirical statement, by others as a normative one.) Still other complications arise from the differential rewards and opportunities inevitable in any complex society, from the differences in the initial endowment individuals bring into the world, and from the symbolism and fears that so often attend the division of men into ethnic compartments. All these confound the effort to develop a satisfactory theory of democratic equality, and further serve to frustrate the realization of consensus around egalitarian values.

Faith in the political system. Another perspective on the state of ideology and consensus in America may be obtained by observing how people respond to the political system. How do Americans feel about the political and social institutions by which they are ruled? Do they perceive the system as one they can reach and influence? Are they satisfied that it will govern justly and for the common good?

Sample items relating to these questions are contained in Tables 6 and 7. An assessment of the responses, however, is confounded by an ambivalence in our tradition. Few will question that Americans are patriotic and loyal, that they accept the political system as legitimate, and that they are inclined to shy away from radical or extreme movements which aim to alter or to overthrow the constitutional foundations of the system. Yet Americans are also presumed to have a longstanding suspicion of government—a state of mind which some historians trace back to the depredations of George III and to the habits of self-reliance forced upon our ancestors by frontier life.

Table 6. Political Influentials vs. the Electorate: Responses to Items
Expressing Cynicism toward Government and Politics

Items	Political Influentials (N-3020)	General Electorate (N-1484)
	% Agree	
Most politicians are looking out for themselves above all else.	36.3	54.3
Both major parties in this country are controlled by the wealthy and are run for their benefit.	7.9	32.1
Many politicians are bought off by some private interest.	43.0	65.3
I avoid dealing with public officials as much as I can.	7.8	39.3
Most politicians can be trusted to do what they think is best for the country.	77.1	58.9
I usually have confidence that the government will do what is right.	81.6	89.6
The people who really "run" the country do not even get known to the voters.	40.2	60.5
The laws of this country are supposed to benefit all of us equally, but the fact is that they're almost all "rich-man's laws."	8.4	33.3
No matter what the people think, a few people will always run things anyway.	30.0	53.8
Most politicians don't seem to me to really mean what they say.	24.7	55.1
There is practically no connection between what a politician says and what he will do once he gets elected.	21.4	54.0
A poor man doesn't have the chance he deserves in the law courts.	20.3	42.9
Most political parties care only about winning elections and nothing more.	28.3	46.2
All politics is controlled by political bosses.	15.6	45.9

It is impossible in the present context to determine the extent to which the scores contained in these tables signify genuine frustration and political disillusionment and the extent to which they represent familiar and largely ritualistic responses. It is plain, however, that Americans are, verbally at least, both confused and divided in their reactions to the political system. Many feel themselves hopelessly ineffectual politically. Approximately half perceive government and politicans as remote, inaccessible, and largely unresponsive to the electorate's needs or opinions. About the same proportion regard politics as squalid and seamy, as an activity in which the participants habitually practice deception, expediency, and self-aggrandizement. Yet by a curious inconsistency which so frequently frustrates the investigator searching the data for regularities, 89.6 per cent express confidence that the government will do what is right. However strongly they mistrust the men and the procedures through which public policies are fashioned, most voters seem not to be greatly dissatisfied with the outcome. They may be cynical about the operation of the political system, but they do not question its legitimacy.

Table 7. Political Influentials vs. the Electorate: Responses to Items Expressing a Sense of Political Futility

Items	Political Influentials (N=3020)	General Electorate (N=1484)
	% Agree	
It's no use worrying my head about public affairs; I can't do anything about them anyhow.	2.3	20.5
The people who really "run" the country do not even get known to the voters.	40.2	60.5
I feel that my political leaders hardly care what people like myself think or want.	10.9	39.0
Nothing I ever do seems to have any effect upon what happens in politics.	8.4	61.5
Political parties are so big that the average member hasn't got much to say about what goes on.	37.8	67.5
There doesn't seem to be much connection between what I want and what my representative does.	24.0	43.7
It seems to me that whoever you vote for, things go on pretty much the same.	21.1	51.3

Although the influentials do not unanimously endorse American political practices either, they are substantially less suspicious and cynical than is the electorate. Indeed, they have achieved consensus or come close to achieving it on most of the items in the two tables. These results are further borne out by the *scale* scores: only 10.1 per cent of the articulates score "high" on the political cynicism scale, as contrasted with 31.3 per cent of the general population; on political suspiciousness the scores are 9.0 per cent high versus 26.7 per cent; on pessimism they are 12.6 per cent versus 26.7 per cent; and on sense of political futility the influentials score (understandably enough) only 3.1 per cent high compared with 30.2 per cent high for the electorate. The active minority also exhibits a stronger sense of social responsibility than the people do (their respective percentage high scores are 40.7 per cent versus 25.8 per cent) and, as previously noted, they are less tolerant of infractions against ethical political procedures.

Should we not, however, have expected these results as a matter of course, considering that the influentials were selected for study precisely because of their political experience and involvement? Possibly, except that similar (though less pronounced) differences emerge when we distinguish articulates from inarticulates by criteria other than actual political activity. Voters, for example, who have been to college, attained high status occupations or professions, or developed strong intellectual interests are, by a significant margin, also likely to possess more affirmative attitudes toward government, politics, and politicians. They display a greater sense of social and political responsibility, are more optimistic, and are less indulgent of shoddy political methods. The political actives who are highly educated exhibit these attitudes even more strongly. Familiarity, it seems, far from breeding contempt, greatly increases respect, hope and support for the nation's political institutions and practices. Inferential support for this generalization is available from the findings turned up by Almond and Verba in all five countries they investigated in their comparative study of citizenship.

Coherence and consistency of attitudes. So far we have explored the question of ideology and consensus mainly from the point of view of agreement on particular values. This, however, is a minimum criterion. Before one can say that a class or group or nation has achieved consensus around an ideology, one should be satisfied that they understand its values in a coherent and correct way. It is a poor consensus in which generalities and slogans are merely echoed with little appreciation of their significance. It seemed appropriate, therefore, to compare the influentials and voters concerning their information and understanding, the relation of their opinions to their party preferences, and the consistency of their views on public affairs.

To begin with, the influentials are more likely than the electorate to have opinions on public questions. For example, 28 per cent of the public are unable (though a few may only be *unwilling*) to classify themselves as liberal, middle of the road, or conservative; while only 1.1 per cent of the articulates fail to make this classification. Forty-eight percent of the voters, compared to 15 per cent of the actives, do not know in which direction they would turn if the parties were reorganized to reflect ideological differences more clearly. Forty-five per cent of the electorate but only 10.2 per cent of the influentials cannot name any issue that divides the parties. By ratios of approximately three or four to one the electorate is less likely to know which level of government they are mainly interested in, whether they prefer their party to control Congress or the presidency, whether they believe in party discipline and of what type, whether control of the parties should rest at the national or local levels, and so on.

As these and other of our findings suggest, active political involvement heightens one's sense of intellectual order and commitment. This inference is further supported by the data on partisanship. One example may suffice to illustrate the point: when the articulates and the electorate are ranged on a scale assessing their orientation toward 14 current liberal-conservative issues, the political actives tend to bunch up at the extreme ends of the distribution (the Democratic actives at the "liberal" end, the Republican actives at the "conservative" end), while the rank and file supporters of both parties fall more frequently into the middle or conflicted category. The political influentials, in short, display issue orientations that are more partisan and more consistent with their party preferences.

Essentially the same effect is achieved among the general population by increases in education, economic status, or other factors that raise the level of articulateness. College-educated Democrats and Republicans, for example, disagree more sharply on issues than grade school Democrats and Republicans do. Partisan differences are greater between the informed than between the uninformed, between the upper-class supporters of the two parties than between the lower-class supporters, between the "intellectuals" in both parties than between those who rank low on "intellectuality."

Increases in political knowledge or involvement, hence, cause men not so much to waver as to choose sides and to identify more unswervingly with one political tendency or its opposite. Inarticulateness and distance from the sources of political decision increase intellectual uncertainty and evoke political responses that are random rather than systematic. We are thus led by the findings to a pair of conclusions that may at first appear contradictory but that in reality are not: the political class is more united than the electorate on fundamental political values but divides more sharply by party affiliation on the issues which separate the two parties. Both facts—the greater consensus in the one instance and the sharper cleavage in the other—testify to its superior ideological sophistication.

Not only are the articulates more partisan, but they are also more consistent in their views. Their responses to a wide range of political stimuli are to a greater extent intellectually patterned and informed. They are, for example, better able to name reference groups that correspond with their party affiliation and doctrinal orientation: approximately twice as many active Democrats as ordinary Democratic voters name liberal, Democratically oriented organizations as groups they would seek advice from (*e.g.*, trade unions, Farmers Union, etc.); and by equally large or larger ratios they *reject* as sources of advice such conservative or Republican oriented organizations as the NAM, the Farm Bureau, and the Chamber of Commerce. With some variations, similar findings emerge when Republican leaders are compared with Republican voters. If we also take into account the liberal or conservative issue-orientation of the respondents, the differential ability of party leaders and followers to recognize reference groups becomes even more pronounced. Clearly, the political stratum has a better idea than the public has of who its ideological friends and enemies are. The capacity to recognize sympathetic or hostile reference groups is not highly developed among the public at large.

Compared with the influentials, ordinary voters also show up poorly in their ability to classify themselves politically. For example, among Democratic actives who score as "liberals" in their views on issues, 82.2 per cent correctly describe themselves as "liberals," while 16.7 per cent call themselves "middle of the roaders" and only 1.1 per cent misclassify themselves as "conservatives." Among Democratic *voters* who actually hold liberal views, only 37.0 percent are able to label themselves correctly. The disparity is less striking between Republican leaders and followers but bears out no less conclusively that most voters lack the sophistication to recognize and label accurately the tendency of their own political views. Even their choice of party is frequently discrepant with their actual ideological views: as we reported in a previous paper, not only do Democratic and Republican voters hold fairly similar opinions on issues, but the latter's opinions are closer to the opinions of Democratic leaders than to those of their own leaders.

Data we have gathered on patterns of support for individual political leaders yield similar conclusions: the articulates are far better able than the electorate to select leaders whose political philosophy they share. Often, in fact, voters simultaneously approve of two or more leaders who represent widely different outlooks—for example, Joseph McCarthy and Dwight D. Eisenhower. In a similar vein, a surprisingly large number of voters simultaneously score high on a Right Wing scale and a liberal issues scale, or hold other "discrepant" outlooks. Such inconsistencies are not unknown among the political actives either, but they are much less frequent. Not only does the public have less information than the political class but it does not succeed as well in sorting out and relating the information it does possess.

Most of the relationships reported in the foregoing have been tested with education, occupation, and sometimes with other demographic variables controlled, but the introduction of these factors does not change the direction of the findings, although it sometimes affects the magnitude of the scores.

Comparisons of scores for the two samples have also been made with "acquiescent" response-set controlled. Acquiescence affects the results, but does not eliminate the differences reported or alter the direction or significance of the findings.

Summary and Discussion

Several observations can be offered by way of summarizing and commenting upon the data just reported:

(1) American politics is widely thought to be innocent of ideology, but this opinion more appropriately describes the electorate than the active political minority. If American ideology is defined as that cluster of axioms, values and beliefs which have given form and substance to American democracy and the Constitution, the political influentials manifest by comparison with ordinary voters a more developed sense of ideology and a firmer grasp of its essentials. This is evidenced in their stronger approval of democratic ideas, their greater tolerance and regard for proper procedures and citizen rights, their superior understanding and acceptance of the "rules of the game," and their more affirmative attitudes toward the political system in general. The electorate displays a substantial measure of unity chiefly in its support of freedom in the

abstract; on most other features of democratic belief and practice it is sharply divided.

The political views of the influentials are relatively ordered and coherent. As liberals and conservatives, Democrats and Republicans, they take stands on issues, choose reference groups, and express preferences for leaders that are far more consistent than the attitudes and preferences exhibited by the electorate. The latter's opinions do not entirely lack order but are insufficiently integrated to meet the requirements of an ideology. In contrast to the political elite, which tends to be united on basic values but divided on issues by party affiliation (both of which testify to a measure of ideological sophistication), the voters divide on many basic political values and adopt stands on issues with little reference to their party affiliation.

The evidence suggests that it is the articulate classes rather than the public who serve as the major repositories of the public conscience and as the carriers of the Creed. Responsibility for keeping the system going, hence, falls most heavily upon them.

(2) Why should consensus and support for democratic ideology be stronger among the political stratum than among the electorate? The answer plainly has to do with the differences in their political activity, involvement and articulateness.

Some observers complain that Americans have little interest in political ideas because they are exclusively concerned with their own personal affairs. Evidence is becoming available, however, that political apathy and ignorance are also widespread among the populations of other countries and may well be endemic in all societies larger than a city-state. It is difficult to imagine any circumstance, short of war or revolutionary crisis, in which the mass of men will evince more interest in the community's affairs than in their own concerns. This is not because they are selfish, thoughtless, or morally deficient, but because the stimuli they receive from public affairs are relatively remote and intangible. One can scarcely expect ordinary men to respond to them as intensely as they respond to the more palpable stimuli in their own everyday lives, which impinge upon them directly and in ways they can understand and do something about. The aphorism which holds man to be a political animal may be supportable on normative grounds but is scarcely defensible as a description of reality. Political apathy seems for most men the more " natural" state. Although political matters are in a sense "everyone's concern," it is just as unreasonable to hope that all men will sustain a lively interest in politics as it would be to expect everyone to become addicted to chamber music, electronics, poetry, or baseball. Since many voters lack education, opportunity, or even tangible and compelling reasons for busying themselves with political ideas, they respond to political stimuli (if they respond at all) without much reflection or consistency. Their life-styles, furthermore, tend to perpetuate this state of affairs, for they are likely to associate with people like themselves whose political opinions are no more informed or consistent than their own. As inarticulates, they are also inclined to avoid the very activities by which they might overcome their indifference and develop a more coherent point of view.

Many voters, in addition, feel remote from the centers of political decision and experience an acute sense of political futility. They know the political world only as a bewildering labyrinth of procedures and unceasing turmoil in which it is difficult to distinguish the just from the wicked, the deserving from the undeserving. The political questions about which they are asked to have opinions are complex and thorny; every solution is imperfect and exacts its price; measures that benefit some groups invariably aggrieve others. The principles which govern the political process seem vague, recondite and impossible to relate to actual events. All this obviously deters voters from developing ideologically, from acquiring insights into the subtleties of the democratic process, and from achieving consensus even on fundamental values.

Although the influentials face some of the same obstacles, they are better able to overcome them. As a group they are distinguished from the mass of the electorate by their above-average education and economic status, their greater political interest and awareness, and their more immediate access to the command posts of community decision. Many of them participate not only in politics but in other public activities as well. This affords them, among other benefits, a more sophisticated understanding of how the society is run and a more intimate association with other men and women who are alert to political ideas and values. Political concepts and abstractions, alien to the vocabulary of many voters, are for the elite familiar items of everyday discourse.

Consider also that the political stratum is, by almost every social criterion we have examined, more homogeneous than the electorate. This promotes communication among them and increases their chances of converging around a common body of attitudes. As Newcomb has remarked, "The actual consequences of communication, as well as the intended ones, are consensus—increasing." Among many segments of the general population, however, communication on matters of political belief either occurs not at all or is so random and cacophonous as to have little utility for the reinforcement of political values. If Louis Wirth is correct in observing that "the limits of consensus are marked by the range of effective communication," it becomes easier to understand why the active minority achieves consensus more often than the voters do.

Compared with the electorate, whose ordinary members are submerged in an ideological babble of poorly informed and discordant opinions, the members of the political minority inhabit a world in which political ideas are vastly more salient, intellectual consistency is more frequently demanded, attitudes are related to principles, actions are connected to beliefs, "correct" opinions are rewarded and "incorrect" opinions are punished. In addition, as participants in political roles, the actives are compelled (contrary to stereotype) to adopt opinions, to take stands on issues, and to evaluate ideas and events. As *articulates* they are unavoidably exposed to the liberal democratic values which form the main current of our political heritage. The net effect of these influences is to heighten their sensitivity to political ideas and to unite them more firmly behind the values of the American tradition. They may, as a result, be better equipped for the role they are called upon to play in a democracy than the citizens are for *their* role.

The findings furnish little comfort for those who wish to believe that a passion for freedom, tolerance, justice and other democratic values springs spontaneously from the lower depths of the society, and that the plain, homespun, uninitiated yeoman, worker and farmer are the natural hosts of democratic ideology. The mystique of the simple, unworldly, "natural" democrat has been with us since at least the rise of Christianity, and has been assiduously cultivated by Rousseau, Tolstoy, Marx, and numerous lesser writers and social reformers. Usually, the simpler the man, the lower his station in life, and the greater his objective need for equality, the more we have endowed him with a capacity for understanding democracy. We are thus inclined to give the nod to the farmer over the city man, the unlearned over the educated, the poor man over the man of wealth, the "people" over their leaders, the unsophisticated over the sophisticated. Yet everyone of these intuitive expectations turns out, upon investigation, to be questionable or false. Democratic beliefs and habits are obviously not "natural" but must be learned; and they are learned more slowly by men and women whose lives are circumscribed by apathy, ignorance, provincialism and social or physical distance from the centers of intellectual activity. In the absence of knowledge and experience—as we can readily observe from the fidgety course of growth in the newly emerging nations—the presuppositions and complex obligations of democracy, the rights it grants and the self-restraints it imposes, cannot be quickly comprehended. Even in a highly developed democratic nation like the United States, millions of people continue to possess only the most rudimentary understanding of democratic ideology.

(3) While the active political minority affirms the underlying values of democracy more enthusiastically than the people do, consensus among them is far from perfect, and we might well inquire why this is so.

Despite the many forces impelling influentials toward agreement on basic ideological values, counteracting forces are also at work to divide them. Not all influentials are able to comprehend democratic ideas, to apply them to concrete contexts, or to thread their way through the complexities of modern political life. Nor is communication perfect among them either, despite their greater homogeneity. Many things divide them, not least of which are differences in education, conflicting economic and group interests, party competition, factional cleavages and personal political ambitions.

In demonstrating that the influentials are better prepared than the masses to receive and reflect upon political ideas, we run the risk of overstating the case and of exaggerating their capacity for ideological reasoning. Some members of the political class obviously have no more intellectual concern with politics than the masses do; they are in it for "the game," for personal reasons, or for almost any reason except ideology.

Then, too, while most democratic ideas are in their most general form simple enough for almost all members of the elite to understand, they become considerably more puzzling when one sets out to explicate them, to relate them to each other, or to apply them to concrete cases. Only a few of the complications need to be cited to illustrate the point: several of the ideas, such as equality, are either inherently vague or mean different things in different contexts. Some democratic (or constitutional) values turn out in certain situations to be incompatible with other democratic values (*e.g.,* the majority's right to make and enforce the laws at times clashes with individual rights, such as the right to stand on one's religious conscience). As this suggests, democratic ideas and rules of the game are ordinarily encountered not in pure form or in isolation but in substantive contexts that are bound to influence the ways in which we react to them. Many businessmen who consider the regulation of business as an unconstitutional invasion of freedom look upon the regulation of trade unions as a justifiable curb upon lawlessness; trade unionists, needless to say, lean to the opposite view.

Consider, too, what a heavy burden we place upon a man's normal impulses by asking him to submit unconditionally to democratic values and procedures. Compliance with democratic rules of the game often demands an extraordinary measure of forbearance and self-discipline, a willingness to place constraints upon the use of our collective power and to suffer opinions, actions, and groups we regard as repugnant. The need for such self-restraint is for many people intrinsically difficult to comprehend and still more difficult to honor. Small wonder, then, that consensus around democratic values is imperfect, even among the political influentials who are well situated to appreciate their importance.

(4) We turn now to the most crucial question suggested by the research findings, namely, what significance must be assigned to the fact that democratic ideology and consensus are poorly developed among the electorate and only imperfectly realized among the political influentials?

Our first and most obvious conclusion is that, contrary to the familiar claim, a democratic society can survive despite widespread popular misunderstanding and disagreement about basic democratic and constitutional values. The American political system survives and even flourishes under precisely these conditions, and so, we have reason to think, do other viable democracies. What makes this possible is a more conjectural question, though several observations can be offered by way of answering it.

Democratic viability is, to begin with, saved by the fact that those who are most confused about democratic ideas are also likely to be politically apathetic and without significant influence. Their role in the nation's decision process is so small that their "misguided" opinions or non-opinions have little practical consequence for stability. If they contribute little to the vitality of the system, neither are they likely to do much harm. Lipset has pointed out that "apathy undermines consensus," but to this one may add the corollary observation that apathy also furnishes its own partial corrective by keeping the doubters from acting upon their differences. In the United States, at least, their disagreements are *passive* rather than *active*, more the result of political ignorance and indifference than of intellectual conviction or conscious identification with an "alien" political tendency. Most seem not even to be aware of their deviations from the established values. This suggests that there may, after all, be some utility in achieving agreement on large, abstract political sentiments, for it may satisfy men that they share common values when in fact they do not. Not only can this keep conflicts from erupting, but it also permits men who disagree to continue to communicate and thus perhaps to convert their pseudo-consensus on democratic values into a genuine consensus.

I do not mean to suggest, of course, that a nation runs no risks when a large number of its citizens fail to grasp the essential principles on which its constitution is founded. Among Americans, however, the principal danger is not that they will reject democratic ideals in favor of some hostile ideology, but that they will fail to understand the very institutions they believe themselves to be defending and may end up undermining rather than safeguarding them. Our research on "McCarthyism," for example, strongly suggests that popular support for the Senator represented less a conscious rejection of American democratic ideals than a misguided effort to defend them. We found few McCarthy supporters who genuinely shared the attitudes and values associated with his name.

Whether consensus among the influentials is either a necessary or sufficient condition for democratic stability is not really known. Since the influentials act, make public decisions, are more organized, and take political ideas more seriously, agreement among them on constitutional values is widely thought to be essential for viability. At present, however, we do not have enough information (or at least we do not have it in appropriately organized form) to state with satisfactory precision what the actual relation is between elite consensus and democratic stability. Some democratic governments, *e.g.,* Weimar Germany, crumbled when faced with ideological conflicts among their political classes; others, *e.g.,* post-war Italy and France, have until now managed to weather pronounced ideological cleavages. The opinion has long prevailed that consensus is needed to achieve stability, but the converse may be the more correct formulation, *i.e.,* that so long as conditions remain stable, consensus is not required; it becomes essential only when social conditions are disorganized. Consensus may strengthen democratic viability, but its absence in an otherwise stable society need not be fatal or even particularly damaging.

It should also be kept in mind that the existence of intellectual disagreements—even among the influentials—does not necessarily mean that they will be expressed or acted upon. In the United States (and doubtless elsewhere as well), numerous influences are at work to prevent ideological cleavages from assuming an important role in the nation's political life. This is certainly the tendency of such political institutions as federalism, checks and balances, separation of powers, bicameralism, the congressional committee system, the judiciary's practice of accomodating one discrepant law to another, and a system of elections more often fought around local issues and personalities than around urgent national questions. Our two-party system also functions to disguise or soften the genuine disagreements that distinguish active Democrats from active Republicans. The American social system contributes to the same end, for it is a model of the pluralistic society, a profuse collection of diverse groups, interests and organizations spread over a vast and variegated territory. Consensus in such a society becomes difficult to achieve, but by the same token its absence can also more easily be survived. The complexities of a highly pluralistic social and political order tend to diminish the impact of intellectual differences, to compel compromise, and to discourage the holders of divergent views from crystalizing into intransigent doctrinal camps. Thus it seems, paradoxically enough, that the need for consensus on democratic rules of the game increases as the conflict among competing political tendencies becomes sharper, and declines as their differences become more diffused. Italy, by this reasoning, has greater need of consensus than the United States, but has less chance of achieving it. A democratic nation may wisely prefer the American model to the Italian, though what is ideally desired, as Lipset observes, is a balance between cleavage and consensus—the one to give reality and force to the principle of opposition, the other to furnish the secure framework within which that principle might be made continuously effective. Countervailing power within a structure of shared political values would, by this logic, be the optimal condition for the maintenance of a democratic society.

(5) But even giving this much weight to consensus may exaggerate the role which intellectual factors play in the attainment of democratic stability. The temptation to assign a controlling influence to the place of ideas in the operation of democracy is very great. Partly this results from our tendency to confuse the textbook model of democracy with the reality and to assume the high order of rationality in the system that the model presupposes (*e.g.,* an alert citizenry aware of its rights and duties, cognizant of the basic rules, exercising consent, enjoying perfect information and choosing governors after carefully weighing their qualifications, deliberating over the issues, etc.). It is not my purpose to ridicule this model but to underscore the observation that it can easily mislead us into placing more weight than the facts warrant upon cognitive elements— upon ideas, values, rational choice, consensus, etc.—as the cementing forces of a democratic society. An *ad hominem* consideration may also be relevant here: as intellectuals and students of politics, we are disposed both by training and sensibility to take political ideas seriously and to assign central importance to them in the operation of the state. We are therefore prone to forget that most people take them less seriously than we do, that they pay little attention to issues, rarely worry about the consistency of their opinions, and spend little or no time thinking about the values, presuppositions, and implications which distinguish one political orientation from another. If the viability of a democracy were to depend upon the satisfaction of these intellectual activities, the prognosis would be very grim indeed.

Research from many different lines of inquiry confirms unequivocally that the role heretofore assigned to ideas and to intellectual processes in general has been greatly exaggerated and cannot adequately explain many political phenomena which, on *a priori* grounds, we have expected them to explain. Witness, for example, the research on the non-rational factors which govern the voting decision, on the effects—or rather the non-effects—of ideology on the loyalty and fighting effectiveness of German and American soldiers, on the differences between the views of party leaders and followers, on the influence of personality on political belief, and on group determinants of perception. We now have evidence that patriotism and the strength of one's attachment to a political community need not depend upon one's approval of its intellectual, cultural, or political values. Indeed, our present research clearly confirms that the men and women who express "patriotism" in extreme or chauvinistic form usually have the least knowledge and understanding of American democratic ideals, institutions, and practices.

Abundant anecdotal data from the observation of dictatorial and other nations further corroborates the conclusion that men may become attached to a party, a community, or a nation by forces that have nothing to do with ideology or consensus. Many of these forces are so commonplace that we often neglect them, for they include family, friends, home, employment, property, religion, ethnic attachments, a common language, and familiar surroundings and customs. These may lack the uplifting power of some political doctrines, but their ability to bind men to a society and its government may nevertheless be great. This observation, of course, is less likely to hold for the intelligentsia than for the inarticulates, but even the political behavior of intellectuals is never governed exclusively by appeals to the mind.

The effect of ideas on democratic viability may also be diminished by the obvious reluctance of most men to press their intellectual differences to the margin and to debate questions that may tear the community apart. So long as no urgent reason arises for bringing such differences to the surface, most men will be satisfied to have them remain dormant. Although there are men and women who are exceptions to this generalization, and who cannot bear to leave basic questions unresolved, they are likely to be few, for both the principles and practices of an "open society" strongly reinforce tolerance for variety, contingency and ambiguity in matters of belief and conscience. As our data on freedom of opinion suggest, few Americans expect everyone to value the same things or to hold identical views on public questions. The tendency to ignore, tolerate, or play down differences helps to create an illusion of consensus which for many purposes can be as serviceable as the reality.

(6) To conclude, as we have in effect, that ideological awareness and consensus are overvalued as determinants of democratic viability is not to imply that they are of no importance. While disagreements among Americans on fundamental values have tended to be passive and, owing to apathy and the relative placidity of our politics, easily tolerated; while they do not follow party lines and are rarely insinuated into the party struggle; and while no extremist movement has yet grown large enough to challenge effectively the governing principles of the American Constitution, this happy state of affairs is not permanently guaranteed. Fundamental differences could *become* activated by political and economic crises; party differences could *develop* around fundamental constitutional questions, as they have in France and other democracies; and powerful extremist movements are too familiar a phenomenon of modern political life to take for granted their eternal absence from the American scene.

Obviously a democratic nation also pays a price for an electorate that is weakly developed ideologically. Lacking the intellectual equipment to assess complex political events accurately, the unsophisticated may give support to causes that are contrary to their own or to the national interest. In the name of freedom, democracy, and the Constitution, they may favor a McCarthy, join the

John Birch Society, or agitate for the impeachment of a Supreme Court Justice who has worked unstintingly to uphold their constitutional liberties. They may also have difficulty discriminating political integrity from demagoguery, maturity and balanced judgment from fanaticism, honest causes from counterfeits. Our findings on the attitudes shown by ordinary Americans toward "extreme" political beliefs (Left Wing beliefs, Right Wing beliefs, totalitarianism, isolationism, etc.) verify that the possibilities just cited are not merely hypothetical. Those who have the least understanding of American politics subscribe least enthusiastically to its principles, and are most frequently "misled" into attacking constitutional values while acting (as they see it) to defend them.

There is, however, reason to believe that ideological sophistication and the general acceptance of liberal democratic values are increasing rather than declining in the United States. Extreme ideological politics of the type associated with Marxism, fascism and other doctrinaire networks of opinion may be waning, as many sociologists believe, but the same observation does not hold for the influence of democratic ideas. On the contrary, democratic ideology in the United States, linked as it is with the articulate classes, gives promise of growing as the articulate class grows. Many developments in recent American life point to an increase in "articulateness": the extraordinary spread of education, rapid social mobility, urbanization, the proliferation of mass media that disseminate public information, the expansion of the middle class, the decline in the size and number of isolated rural groups, the reduction in the proportion of people with submarginal living standards, the incorporation of foreign and minority groups into the culture and their increasing entrance into the professions, and so on. While these developments may on the one side have the effect of reducing the tensions and conflicts on which extreme ideologies feed, they are likely on the other side to beget a more articulate population and a more numerous class of political influentials, committed to liberal democracy and aware of the rights and obligations which attend that commitment.

Working Class Authoritarianism

Seymour Martin Lipset

Democracy and the Lower Classes

The poorer strata everywhere are more liberal or leftist on economic issues; they favor more welfare state measures, higher wages, graduated income taxes, support of trade-unions, and so forth. But when liberalism is defined in noneconomic terms—as support of civil liberties, internationalism, etc.—the correlation is reversed. The more well-to-do are more liberal, the poorer are more intolerant. . . .

Low-status groups are also less apt to participate in formal organizations, read fewer magazines and books regularly, possess less information on public affairs, vote less, and, in general, take less interest in politics. The available evidence suggests that each of these attributes is related to attitudes toward democracy. The 1953 UNESCO analysis of German data found that, at every occupational level, those who belonged to voluntary associations were more likely to favor a multi-party system than a one-party one. American findings, too, indicate that authoritarians "do not join many community groups" as compared with nonauthoritarians. And it has been discovered that people poorly informed on public issues are more likely to be both *more liberal* on economic issues and *less liberal* on noneconomic ones. Nonvoters and those less interested in political matters are much more intolerant and xenophobic than those who vote and have political interests.

Table 1.   The Relationship between Occupation, Education, and
Support of a Democratic Party System in Germany—1953.
(Per Cent Favoring the Existence of Several Parties)

| | Educational Level | |
| | Elementary School | High School or Higher |
Occupation		
Farm Laborers	29 (59)	—
Manual Workers	43 (1439)	52 (29)
Farmers	43 (381)	67 (9)
Lower White Collar	50 (273)	68 (107)
Self-employed Business	53 (365)	65 (75)
Upper White Collar	58 (86)	69 (58)
Officials (Govt.)	59 (158)	78 (99)
Professions	56 (18)	68 (38)

The "hard core" of "chronic know-nothings" comes disproportionately from the less literate, lower socioeconomic groups, according to a study by two American social psychologists, Herbert Hyman and Paul Sheatsley. These people are not only uninformed, but "harder to reach, no matter what the level or nature of the information." Here is another hint of the complex character of the relationship between education, liberalism, and status. Noneconomic liberalism is not a simple matter of acquiring education and information; it is at least in part a basic attitude which is actively discouraged by the social situation of lower-status persons. As Genevieve Knupfer, an American psychiatrist, has pointed out in her revealing "Portrait of the Underdog," "economic underprivilege is psychological underprivilege: habits of submission, little access to sources of information, lack of verbal facility . . . appear to produce a lack of self-confidence which increases the unwillingness of the low-status person to participate in many phases of our predominantly middle-class culture. . . ."

These characteristics also reflect the extent to which the lower strata are *isolated* from the activities, controversies, and organizations of democratic society—an isolation which prevents them from acquiring the sophisticated and complex view of the political structure which makes understandable and necessary the norms of tolerance.

In this connection it is instructive to examine once again, as extreme cases, those occupations which are most isolated, in every sense, from contact with the world outside their own group. Manual workers in "isolated occupations" which require them to live in one-industry towns or areas—miners, maritime workers, forestry workers, fishermen, and sheepshearers—exhibit high rates of Communist support in most countries.

Similarly, as all public opinion surveys show, the rural population, both farmers and laborers, tends to oppose civil liberties and multi-party systems more than any other occupational group. Election surveys indicate that farm owners have been among the strongest supporters of fascist parties, while farm workers, poor farmers, and share-croppers have given even stronger backing to the Communists than has the rest of labor in countries like Italy, France, and India.

The same social conditions are associated with middle-class authoritarianism. The groups which have been most prone to support fascist and other middle-class extremist ideologies have been, in addition to farmers and peasants, the small businessmen of the smaller provincial communities—groups which are also isolated from "cosmopolitan" culture and are far lower than any other non-manual-labor group in educational attainment.

A second and no less important factor predisposing the lower classes toward authoritarianism is a relative lack of economic and psychological security. The lower one goes on the socioeconomic ladder, the greater economic uncertainty one finds. White-collar workers, even those who are not paid more than skilled manual workers, are less likely to suffer the tensions created by fear of loss of income. Studies of marital instability indicate that this is related to lower income and income insecurity. Such insecurity will of course affect the individual's politics and attitudes. High states of tension require immediate alleviation, and this is frequently found in the venting of hostility against a scapegoat and the search for a short-term solution by support of extremist groups. Research indicates that the unemployed are less tolerant toward minorities than the employed, and more likely to be Communists if they are workers, or fascists if they are middle class. Industries which have a high rate of Communists in their ranks also have high economic instability.

The lower classes' insecurities and tensions which flow from economic instability are reinforced by their particular patterns of family life. There is a great deal of direct frustration and aggression in the day-to-day lives of members of the lower classes, both children and adults. A comprehensive review of the many studies of child-rearing patterns in the United States completed in the past twenty-five years reports that their "most consistent finding" is the "more frequent use of physical punishment by working-class parents. The middle class, in contrast, resorts to reasoning, isolation, and . . . 'love-oriented' techniques of discipline. . . . Such parents are more likely to overlook offenses, and when they do punish they are less likely to ridicule or inflict physical pain." A further link between such child-rearing practices and adult hostility and authoritarianism is suggested by the finding of two investigations in Boston and Detroit that physical punishments for aggression, characteristic of the working class, tend to increase rather than decrease aggressive behavior.

Making of an Authoritarian

.

To sum up, the lower-class individual is likely to have been exposed to punishment, lack of love, and a general atmosphere of tension and aggression since early childhood—all experiences which tend to produce deep-rooted hostilities expressed by ethnic prejudice, political authoritarianism, and chiliastic transvaluational religion. His educational attainment is less than that of men with higher socioeconomic status, and his association as a child with others of similar background not only fails to stimulate his intellectual interests but also creates an atmosphere which prevents his educational experience from increasing his general social sophistication and his understanding of different groups and ideas. Leaving school relatively early, he is surrounded on the job by others with a similarly restricted cultural, educational, and family background. Little external influence impinges on his limited environment. From early childhood, he has sought immediate gratifications, rather than engaged in activities which might have long-term rewards. The logic of both his adult employment and his family situation reinforces this limited time perspective. As the sociologist C. C. North has put it, isolation from heterogeneous environments, characteristic of low status, operates to "limit the source of information, to retard the development of efficiency in judgment and reasoning abilities, and to confine the attention to more trivial interests in life."

All of these characteristics produce a tendency to view politics and personal relationships in black-and-white terms, a desire for immediate action, an impatience with talk and discussion, a lack of interest in organizations which have a long-range perspective, and a readiness to follow leaders who offer a demonological interpretation of the evil forces (either religious or political) which are conspiring against him.

It is interesting that Lenin saw the character of the lower classes, and the tasks of those who would lead them, in somewhat these terms. He specified as the chief task of the Communist parties the leadership of the broad masses, who are "slumbering, apathetic, hidebound, inert, and dormant." These masses, said Lenin, must be aligned for the "final and decisive battle" (a term reminiscent of Armageddon) by the party which alone can present an uncompromising and unified view of the world, and an immediate program for drastic change. In contrast to "effective" Communist leadership, Lenin pointed to the democratic parties and their leadership as "vacillating, wavering, unstable" elements—a characterization that is probably valid for any political group lacking ultimate certainty in its program and willing to grant legitimacy to opposition groups.

The political outcome of these predispositions, however, is not determined by the multiplicity of factors involved. Isolation, a punishing childhood, economic and occupational insecurities, and a lack of sophistication are conducive to withdrawal, or even apathy, and to strong mobilization of hostility. The same underlying factors which predispose individuals toward support of extremist movements under certain conditions may result in total withdrawal from political activity and concern under other conditions. In "normal" periods, apathy is most frequent among such individuals, but they can be activated by a crisis, especially if it is accompanied by strong millennial appeals.

The Fear of Equality

Robert E. Lane

People Deserve Their Status

If one accepts the view that this is a land of opportunity in which merit will find a way, one is encouraged to accept the status differences of society. But it is more than logic that impels our men to accept these differences. There are satisfactions of identification with the going social order; it is easier to accept differences one calls "just" than those that appear "unjust"; there are the very substantial self-congratulatory satisfactions of comparison with those lower on the scale. Thus this theme of "just desserts" applies to one's own group, those higher, and those lower.

So Kuchinsky says: "If you're a professor, I think you're entitled to get what you deserve. I'm a roofer and I shouldn't be getting what you're getting." Furthermore, confidence in the general equity of the social order suggests that the rewards of one's own life are proportionate to ability, effort, and the wisdom of previous decisions. On ability, Costa, a machine operator, says:

> I believe anybody that has the potential to become a scientific man, or a professor, or a lawyer, or a doctor, should have the opportunity to pursue it, but there's a lot of us that are just made to run a machine in a factory. No matter what opportunities some of us might have had, we would never have reached the point where we could become people of that kind. I mean, everybody isn't Joe DiMaggio.

And on the wisdom of earlier decisions, Johnson, the electric-utility mechanic, says:

> I don't consider myself the lower class. In between someplace. But I could have been a lot better off but through my own foolishness, I'm not. [Here he refers back to an earlier account of his life.] What causes poverty? Foolishness. When I came out of the service, my wife had saved a few dollars and I had a few bucks. I wanted to have a good time. I'm throwing money away like water. Believe me, had I used my head right, I could have had a house. I don't feel sorry for myself—what happened, happened, you know. Of course you pay for it.

But the most usual mistake or deficiency accounting for the relatively humble position is failure to continue one's education owing to lack of family pressure

("They should have made me"), or youthful indiscretion, or the demands of the family for money, or the depression of the thirties.

Just as they regard their own status as deserved, so also do they regard the status of the more eminently successful as appropriate to their talents. Rapuano, the packinghouse clerk, reports:

> Your income—if you're smart, and your ability calls for a certain income, that's what you should earn. If your ability is so low, why, hell, then you should earn the low income. ["Do you think income is proportionate to ability now?"] I would say so. Yes.

But there is a suggestion in many of the interviews that even if the income is divorced from talent and effort, in some sense it is appropriate. Consider Sokolsky again, a machine operator and part-time janitor, discussing the tax situation:

> Personally, I think taxes are too hard. I mean a man makes, let's say $150,000. Well, my God, he has to give up half of that to the government—which I don't think is right. For instance if a man is fortunate enough to win the Irish Sweepstakes, he gets 150—I think he has about $45,000 left. I don't think that's right.

Even if life is a lottery, the winner should keep his winnings. And DeAngelo, a machine operator, comes spontaneously to the same conclusion:

> I think everybody needs a little [tax] relief. I mean, I know one thing, if I made a million dollars and the government took nine-tenths of it—boy, I'd cry the blues. I can't see that. If a man is smart enough to make that much, damn it, he's got a right to holler. I'm with the guy all the way.

Because he is "smart enough" to make the money, it is rightfully his. Surely, beyond the grave, there is a specter haunting Marx.

The concept of "education" is the key to much of the thinking on social class and personal status. In a sense, it is a "natural" because it fits so neatly into the American myth of opportunity and equality, and provides a rationale for success and failure that does minimum damage to the souls of those who did not go to college. Thus in justifying their own positions, sometimes with reference to the interview situation, my clients imply, "If I had gone to college (like you), I would be higher up in this world." Costa, a machine operator, speaks this theme:

> Now, what would be the advantage of you going twenty years to school so you wind up making $10,000 a year and me going eight years to school, making $10,000? You would be teaching the

young men of tomorrow, the leaders of tomorrow, and I would be running a machine. You would have a lot more responsibility to the country as a whole than I would have. Why shouldn't you be rewarded in proportion?

McNamara, a mild-mannered bookkeeper who went to night school to get his training in accounting and bookkeeping, emphasizes education in response to the question, "Do you think it's easy or hard to get from one class to another?"

> Well, I think it's hard because . . . not because of the class itself, or what the influence they have on you, but you just seem to reach a certain point, and if you don't have it, you just don't—you don't make the grade. I've found that to be true. I always seem to be one step away from a good spot. And it's no one's fault—it's my fault. I just don't have the education—just don't—just don't have what it takes to take that step.

And Sokolsky, machine operator and part-time janitor, says, in justification of income differences:

> A man that gets out of eighth grade—I don't think he would have the ability to do the job as a man that got out of college.

But later, he says, of politicians and businessmen:

> If a man with more education has been in politics, he should get the job, but if there's a man that, let's say, just got out of high school, and he's been around in politics all his life, I think he should have a chance too. It's how good he is. There's some big business people who just haven't got it. [But] there could be some men with a gift of gab—maybe just out of eighth grade—they could sell anything.

What is it about education that justifies differences in income? In the above interviews it is clear that education is thought to increase skills that should be suitably rewarded. Furthermore, it appears that the time necessary for educational preparation deserves some reward—a recurrent theme. With education goes responsibility—and responsibility should be rewarded. But there is also some suggestion in the interview material that the pain and hard (unpleasant) work associated with going to school deserves compensation. People who did not like school themselves may be paying homage to those who could stick it out. It is a question whether O'Hara, a maintenance mechanic, implies this when he says:

> I think a person that is educated deserves more than somebody that isn't. Somebody who really works for his money really deserves it more than somebody that's lazy and just wants to hang around.

In this and other ways, education serves as a peg on which to hang status; and, like "blood," whether a person got the education or not is not his "fault," or at least it is only the fault of an irresponsible youth, not a grown man.

Deprivation of a Meritorious Elite

It is comforting to have the "natural leaders" of a society well entrenched in their proper place. If there were equality there would no longer be such an elite to supervise and take care of people—especially "me." Thus Woodside, the railroad guard, reports:

> I think anybody that has money—I think their interest is much wider than the regular workingman. . . . And therefore I think that the man with the money is a little bit more educated, for the simple reason he has the money, and he has a much wider view of life—because he's in the knowledge of it all the time.

Here and elsewhere in the interview, one senses that Woodside is glad to have such educated, broad-gauged men in eminent positions. He certainly opposes the notion of equality of income. Something similar creeps into Johnson's discussion of social classes. He feels that the upper classes, who "seem to be very nice people," are "willing to lend a helping hand—to listen to you. I would say they'd help you out more than the middle class [man] would help you out even if he was in a position to help you out." Equality, then, would deprive society, and oneself, of a group of friendly, wise, and helpful people who occupy the social eminences.

The Loss of the Goals of Life

But most important of all, equality, at least equality of income, would deprive people of the goals of life. In this they are like the working class of Middletown: "Its drives are largely those of the business class: both are caught up in the tradition of a rising standard of living and lured by the enticements of salesmanship." Every one of the fifteen clients with whom I spent my evenings for seven months believed that equality of income would deprive men of their incentive to work, achieve, and develop their skills. These answers ranged, in their sophistication and approach, across a broad field. The most highly educated man in the sample, Farrel, answers the question "How would you feel if everyone received the same income in our society?" by saying:

> I think it would be kind of silly. . . . Society, by using income as a reward technique, can often insure that the individuals will put forth their best efforts.

He does not believe, for himself, that status or income are central to motivation—but for others, they are. Woodside, whose main concern is not the vistas of wealth and opportunity of the American dream, but rather whether he can get a good pension if he should have to retire early, comes forward as follows:

> I'd say that [equal income] –that is something that's pretty–I think it would be a dull thing, because life would be accepted–or it would–rather we'd go stale. There would be no initiative to be a little different, or go ahead.

Like Woodside, Flynn, a white-collar worker, responds with a feeling of personal loss–the idea of such an equality of income would make him feel "very mad." Costa, whose ambitions in life are most modest, holds that equality of income "would eliminate the basic thing about the wonderful opportunity you have in this country." Then for a moment the notion of his income equaling that of the professional man passes pleasantly through his mind: "Don't misunderstand me–I like the idea"; then again, "I think it eliminates the main reason why people become engineers and professors and doctors."

Rapuano, whose worries have given him ulcers, projects himself into a situation where everyone receives the same income, in this case a high one:

> If everyone had the same income of a man that's earning $50,000 a year, and he went to, let's say ten years of college to do that, why, hell, I'd just as soon sit on my ass as go to college and wait till I could earn $50,000 a year, too. Of course, what the hell am I going to do to earn $50,000 a year–now that's another question.

But however the question is answered, he is clear that guaranteed equal incomes would encourage people to sit around on their anatomies and wait for their paychecks. But he would like to see some leveling, particularly if doctors, whom he hates, were to have their fees and incomes substantially reduced.

That These Sacrifices Shall Not Have
Been in Vain

The men I talked to were not at the bottom of the scale; not at all. They were stable breadwinners, churchgoers, voters, family men. They achieved this position in life through hard work and sometimes bitter sacrifices. They are distinguished from the lower classes through their initiative, zeal, and responsibility, their willingness and ability to postpone pleasures or to forego them entirely. In their control of impulse and desire they have absorbed the Protestant ethic. At least six of them have two jobs and almost no leisure. In answering questions on "the last time you remember having a specially good time," some of them must go back ten to fifteen years. Nor are their good times remarkable for their spontaneous fun and enjoyment of life. Many of them do not like their jobs, but stick to them because of family responsibilities–and they do not know what else they would rather do. In short, they have sacrificed their hedonistic inclinations, given up good times, and expended their energy and resources in order to achieve and maintain their present tenuous hold on respectability and middle status.

Now, in such a situation to suggest that men be equalized and the lower orders raised and one's own hard-earned status given to them as a right and not a reward for effort seems to them desperately wrong. In the words of my research assistant, David Sears, "Suppose the Marshall Plan had provided a block and tackle to Sisyphus after all these years. How do you think he would have felt?" Sokolsky, Woodside, and Dempsey have rolled the stone to the top of the hill so long, they despise the suggestion that it might have been in vain. Or even worse, that their neighbors at the foot of the hill might have the use of a block and tackle.

The World Would Collapse

As a corollary to the view that life would lose its vigor and its savor with equality of income, there is the image of an equalitarian society as a world running down, a chaotic and disorganized place to live. The professions would be decimated: "People pursue the higher educational levels for a reason—there's a lot of rewards, either financial or social," says Costa. Sullivan says, "Why should people take the headaches of responsible jobs if the pay didn't meet the responsibilities?" For the general society, Flynn, a white-collar man, believes that "if there were no monetary incentive involved, I think there'd be a complete loss. It would stop all development—there's no doubt about it." McNamara, a bookkeeper, sees people then reduced to a dead level of worth: with equal income "the efforts would be equal and pretty soon we would be worth the same thing." In two contrasting views, both suggesting economic disorganization, Woodside believes, "I think you'd find too many men digging ditches, and no doctors," while Rapuano believes men would fail to dig ditches or sewers, "and where the hell would we be when we wanted to go to the toilet?"

Only a few took up the possible inference that this was an attractive but impractical ideal—and almost none followed up the suggestion that some equalization of income, if not complete equality, would be desirable. The fact of the matter is that these men, by and large, prefer an inequalitarian society, and even prefer a society graced by some men of great wealth. As they look out upon the social scene, they feel that an equalitarian society would present them with too many problems of moral adjustment, which they fear and dislike. But perhaps, most important, their life goals are structured around achievement and success in monetary terms. If these were taken away, life would be a desert. These men view the possibility of an equalitarian world as a paraphrased version of Swinburne's lines on Jesus Christ: "Thou hast conquered, O pale Equalitarian; the world has grown grey from thy breath."

Mass Behavior

William Kornhauser

Mass Behavior

Mass behavior is a form of collective behavior exhibiting the following characteristics. (a) *The focus of attention is remote from personal experience and daily life.* Remote objects are national and international issues or events, abstract symbols, and whatever else is known only through the mass media. Of course, not *any* concern for remote objects is a manifestation of mass behavior. Only when that concern leads to direct and activist modes of response can we speak of mass behavior. However, merely by virtue of the fact that mass behavior always involves remote objects certain consequences are likely to follow. Concern for remote objects tends to lack the definiteness, independence, sense of reality, and responsibility to be found in concern for proximate objects. The sphere of proximate objects consists of things that directly concern the individual:

> his family, his business dealings, his hobbies, his friends and enemies, his township or ward, his class, church, trade union or any other social group of which he is an active member—the things under his personal observation, the things which are familiar to him independently of what his newspaper tells him, which he can directly influence or manage and for which he develops the kind of responsibility that is induced by a direct relation to the favorable or unfavorable effects of a course of action.

The sense of reality and responsibility declines as the object of concern becomes more remote:

> Now this comparative definiteness of volition and rationality of behavior does not suddenly vanish as we move away from those concerns of daily life in the home and in business which educate and discipline us. In the realm of public affairs there are sectors that are more within the reach of the citizen's mind than others. This is true, first, of local affairs. Even there we find a reduced power of discerning facts, a reduced preparedness to act upon them, a reduced sense of responsibility. . . . Second, there are many national issues that concern individuals and groups so directly and unmistakably as to evoke volitions that are genuine and definite enough. The most important instance is afforded by issues involving immediate and personal pecuniary profit to individual voters and groups of voters. . . . However, when we move still farther away from the private concerns of the family and the business office into those regions of national and international affairs that lack a direct and unmistakable link with those private concerns, individual volition, command of facts and method of inference soon [decline].

(b) *The mode of response to remote objects is direct.* The lessening of the sense of reality and responsibility and effective volition with the greater remoteness of the focus of attention has particularly marked consequences when the mode of response is direct, rather than being mediated by several intervening layers of social relations. People act directly when they do not engage in discussion on the matter at hand, and when they do not act through groups in which they are capable of persuading and being persuaded by their fellows.

At times, people may act directly by grasping those means of action which lie immediately to hand. They may employ various more or less coercive measures against those individuals and groups who resist them. For example, when large